I0813199

'More demanding than hell, this is parenting purgatory for authentic women who've put their lives on hold to be mummy. Lou makes mums feel SEEN in the shadow of their children, workload... and famous husbands.'

KATHERINE RYAN

'I love it. Why has no one written this book before? We bloody need this book.'

FEARNE COTTON

'Lou writes with such candour and honesty about mum'ing and life; she's made me laugh and cry at the same time – what I call crafting. Read this book immediately.'

ZOE BALL

'Being the default parent is a joyous privilege and the heaviest burden. Lou just gets it. This book will resonate with so many parents who have the family they always wanted but sometimes feel they've had to sacrifice their sense of self worth to get it. A brilliant, comforting and funny read for any default parent, who – after a day of fish fingers and swimming lessons – has whispered to themselves, "I just want to feel important again..." .'

ELLIE TAYLOR

'Lou is a proper mum who totally gets it! This book is laugh-out-loud funny and keeps it real about just how bonkers and hard parenting can be. Honestly you'll be nodding, crying and cackling all at the same time. I loved it.'

ALISON HAMMOND

'Who knew? Maybe I'm the default parent. This book is hilarious and full of common sense.'

JO BRAND

'Lou is certainly an expert on all things parenting; not only has she raised two wonderful children she has also put up with her husband Rob, who has been teething for 38 years.'

MICHAEL MCINTYRE

'This book needed to exist. It's a witty and wise snapshot of how parenting works in the 21st century and Lou writes like she parents, with humour, empathy, joy and a skill most of us can only dream of.'

JOSH WIDDICOMBE

'Funny, articulate, reflective and honest: it's like sitting down with your bestie for a proper mumlife debrief. It's a non-judgemental hand in the dark, an acknowledgement of what it is to be the default parent and a reminder that we're all just trying to do our best.'

GIOVANNA FLETCHER

'A fun and funny polemic on something deadly serious.'

SARA PASCOE

LESSONS FROM A DEFAULT PARENT

LOU BECKETT

LESSONS FROM A DEFAULT PARENT

Surviving the front line of family life

(without losing your sh*t)

First published in Great Britain in 2026 by
DK RED, an imprint of
Dorling Kindersley Limited
20 Vauxhall Bridge Road,
London SW1V 2SA

The authorised representative in the EEA is
Dorling Kindersley Verlag GmbH. Arnulfstr. 124,
80636 Munich, Germany

10 9 8 7 6 5 4 3 2 1
001–351368-Feb/2026

Cover design and illustration by Anna Morrison

A CIP catalogue record for this book
is available from the British Library.
ISBN: 978-0-2417-6291-2

Printed and bound in the United Kingdom

www.dk.com

This book was made with Forest Stewardship Council™ certified paper – one small step in DK's commitment to a sustainable future. Learn more at **www.dk.com/uk/information/sustainability**

To all the parents out there trying to find themselves again,
this is for you.

CONTENTS

INTRODUCTION

THE MOTHER OF ALL CAVEATS

Default: adjective [ADJECTIVE noun] A default situation is what exists or happens unless someone or something changes it.[1]

Let me ask you a question: if you wanted to go for a drink on a Thursday night, how many people would you have to text?

OK, let's try another one: what uniform is your child wearing tomorrow?

One more for fun? What's your child doing for their birthday this year? Who is coming to the party and what's going in the party bags?

If your answer to the first question is 'Huh?', to the second: 'No idea' and to the third: 'I don't know any of their friends' names', then the chances are you are not the default parent. Congratulations.

In fact, it's likely that you are co-parenting with someone who has to text a small army to go out for one quick drink, knows precisely what kit and permission slip your child needs for school on any given day *and* has calculated the exact proportion of sugar to plastic junk that is going in your child's party bag.

If you *did* know the answer to all the above questions, then to the surprise of absolutely not you, you're the default parent!

For clarity (and this is something I feel strongly about), the default parent can be anyone: mums, dads, parents of all flavours. But, by and large, it's often the mums and women who are bearing the brunt of the mental and physical load of keeping a family functioning.

As I was writing this book, it occurred to me that maybe I'm just really lazy and fundamentally unsuited to being a mum – that maybe everyone else is coping just fine and I'm the only one who feels like they're doing the majority of the parenting and struggling to work out who I am now. So, before I wrote an entire book exposing myself, I did some research and it turns out the UK government helpfully published a study in 2021 looking at the gender differences in childcare responsibilities. I won't bore you with the minutiae of the data because who needs that when you're also trying to do the school run and feed the dogs, but to give you the headlines:

- Mothers were *'more likely to be caring for children at any point in the week or weekend'* than fathers.

- Even where mothers have returned to work either full or part time it still found that *'irrespective of their working time, mothers spent a significantly larger amount of time caring than fathers on weekdays'*.

- Even when men are engaging in childcare they are *'more likely to do so jointly with the mother'* and *'take on the more enjoyable enrichment childcare, mainly at the weekend'*.

- *'This leaves most of the routine care of children to mothers, especially on weekdays … what is more, we saw a surprising number of fathers who did not take part in giving* any *childcare'*.[2]

Before we hear the rallying cry of the 'not all men' brigade coming over the hill, *of course* it's not all men, but there's not much debate left in the data: mothers are doing the majority of the childcare, and that's before you even get on to the mental load, which, it turns out, mothers are carrying 70-odd per cent of as well.[3] I'm sure dads in the default position exist; a bit like the perfect black leggings – I know they exist, I just haven't found them yet, but the eternal quest continues.

Data aside, I'm writing from the only experience I have: as a woman and as a mother, but that doesn't preclude your own experiences, whatever they might be. I'm the default parent in an almost painfully stereotypical, heteronormative, two-parent family dynamic. So, while I hope there's something here for everyone, whether that's the absolute heroes managing alone as single parents or even those who are just beginning to question whether parenthood is something they want to embark on at all, most of what I'm talking about is unavoidably from my own perspective of parenting while in a relationship with my co-parent.

I use the terms 'mother', 'mum', 'parent', 'default' and so on pretty interchangeably, but if the themes or content of this book are relevant to you, no matter who you are, what your family looks like or how you identify, feel free to ignore the pronouns or terminology I'm using and swap them out for something more relevant to your situation.

If you're reading this as the non-default to get a sense of how to better support the default parent in your life – welcome. And well done for not luxuriating in the largely blissful ignorance of the default dynamic. Ultimately, whoever you are and whatever your child or parenting situation, hello!

I want to preface everything I'm about to write with the mother of all caveats: I love my husband and I love our children. I love the life I've very wilfully chosen for myself. Nothing I'm about to say in this book negates the love I have for my family or means I would change anything about them. My girls are the total loves of my life and I would fight grizzlies for them. However, the fact that I actively chose to have them doesn't mean that I have to love every single minuscule thing about the impact they've had on my life. There's nothing more frustrating than not being allowed to voice your very valid feelings because someone else thinks you're 'lucky' and delights in shouting that at you the minute you look anything less than deliriously gleeful. Just because you're not eternally and gushingly grateful that must mean you hate your life, or hate your children? *Please*. We have to be allowed to express our feelings about parenthood in their totality without bringing down the ire of the 'what about-ers'. You know the ones; we all know the ones – the people in your life, or in the corners of the internet, who seem incapable of letting you feel something without telling you why you're wrong. So, let's just establish right from the off that loving your children, and this being something you chose, does not mean that things can't be hard, or be difficult, or feel unfair, or, you know, just be a bit downright shit sometimes. I'd like that out there before you embark on reading the exceptionally long whinge I'm about to spew.

This book was born out of a general frustration I was feeling at the new role of 'the default parent' I had found myself filling, one that I'm not entirely sure I ever really signed up for. Because as much as I love my family, the impact of having children on your sense of self is unimaginable. You are no longer your own person, and when you've spent 29 years cultivating the person you were, that's a *slight* adjustment to make to say the least and it's *OK* to say that. And this *slight* adjustment doesn't impact both parents equally.

The physical, mental, social and, to an extent, economic impact of having a child always seems to fall disproportionally on the 'mum' in the dynamic. Of course, I can only really speak to my own experience, but it's one I've seen mirrored to at least some degree time and time again – among my old colleagues at work, among my friends, among my family and among the mums I get chatting to while waiting at whatever absurd child activity is the flavour of that particular month. Default parenting goes beyond the mental load – it's not just the invisible labour that, again, largely women have to perform to keep a family and a home functioning. It's the physicality of being the parent who is responsible for the children most of the time and the impact that inevitably has on our career, identity and personhood. If you are the one who is physically there most of the time, that inevitably lessens the time and space you have to be your own person outside of parenthood.

Unless you've happened upon this book entirely by chance (in which case, hello and nice to meet you!), I'm assuming most of you are here because you know me as one relatively silent quarter of the Parenting Hell podcast of which my husband is part. So, what you've heard of me is almost entirely through Rob's perspective. Which I'm not saying is wrong, but if I've learnt anything by living with a comedian for the last 16 years, it's that the truth is a very subjective thing and anything and anyone – even the mother of your children – is fair game if someone needs to be thrown under a joke bus. Now, that's not to say what you've heard is wrong (I can often be found leaving Rob voice notes seething with rage). However, that's not all I am or, in fact, who I've been. So, if you'll indulge me for a while, I'd like to introduce myself to you, in my totality.

The Other Beckett

Before I became a mum, I spent 29.5 years as a somewhat fully functioning person in my own right. I went to the University of Sheffield and studied History. Well, I started with History and Politics, but in my very first Politics seminar someone answered the question by quoting Latin and I jumped ship pronto. I went on to teach History to boys in a secondary school in Thamesmead in southeast London. If you don't know London, let me just paint the scene for you. I spent 5 years teaching boys aged from 11 to 18 years old, in a comprehensive school sandwiched between Belmarsh high-security prison, an industrial estate shopping centre and a sewage works. I like to think that the years I spent teaching there hardened me up for when my girls became toddlers, but, quite frankly, give me 30 marauding teenage boys over 2 small girls having a meltdown any day.

I loved teaching; it was part of me. I've always needed a vocation of sorts, and I'm not too proud to admit that it made me feel important, like I was maybe making a difference, especially in the school I taught in. I love history and being able to talk about it all day and, dare I say it, even imparting some of that enthusiasm to some of the boys was so fulfilling. I was good at my job as well. I might not have been the best teacher in the world, but I really cared – and I think that came across to the staff I worked with as well as the boys. In part, I think I was able to be the kind of teacher I was because I didn't have children. That might sound like sacrilege in the 21st century when women are constantly told that not only can we have it all, but we're somehow letting down the sisterhood by not having it all – I mean, don't you know our good Emily Davison went under a horse for you? But, realistically, I wouldn't have wanted to go in to teach extra exam sessions on a Saturday or stay after school to teach an excluded pupil once I had the girls. I gave my everything to that job and the boys I taught, and I don't think I have enough everything to go around now I have children.

When I say I gave my everything to that job, I quite literally mean it. For every one lesson I had that was soul-feedingly satisfying, there were at least four where I'd go back to the humanities office and cry into my coffee because I'd spent the last hour feeling like I was shouting into the abyss. Sometimes, no matter how hard you worked, or what you tried, it just wasn't enough. That pupil who was excluded, who I fought for permission to keep teaching in my own time? The one who Rob mentioned in his wedding speech as an example of what a good teacher I was and how I helped kids turn their lives around? Well, he's currently serving life for murder.

Teaching also exacerbated my ulcerative colitis to the point where it was untenable for me to continue. Ulcerative colitis is a chronic disease of the colon, which causes inflammation in the gut. It's a delightful condition causing diarrhoea, cramps and bleeding in the first instance, and then, to add insult to injury, secondary symptoms like anaemia, fatigue, ulcers, swollen joints, osteoporosis and all sorts of other fun things. I was diagnosed in

2007 after completing my final university exams and, over the last decade or so, I've really got an understanding of what can trigger my flares. And what triggers them is stress. I don't know if you've ever stood in front of thirty fifteen-year-olds all shouting and jumping around as three of them throw punches at each other, but Zen it is not. I tried as hard as I could, for as long as I could, to keep on teaching. I stopped eating during the day to try to minimise the severity of the flare during school hours at least and was so full of different tablets that it was a wonder I didn't rattle. After a particularly bad day when I'd had to leave my class by themselves a number of times to run to the staff toilets, having made a split-second decision about which 13-year-old boy to leave in charge, and inevitably returned to escalating levels of chaos each time, culminating with my mum driving 45 minutes to collect me as I couldn't drive myself home, I accepted defeat and initially went part time, followed by eventually leaving completely a year later. I then went to work part time in a pub down the road as I've never not worked and it's important to me, so I thought I'd try something less stressful to see if that helped. I stayed there until I got pregnant and had to call it a day as no one wants someone vomming in between pulling pints. Really puts you off your beer.

I did not go quietly into the night; I loved my teaching job and how it made me feel. I always had something to talk about – a new subject I'd never taught before, a breakthrough with a particular pupil; without fail, either a kid or a parent had always done something deranged. And there was always, *always* Friday-night or end-of-term drinks with a big group of comrades to satisfy your soul. I was part of a team; part of a little teaching gang and I loved it. Then, almost overnight, I went from being too busy, having too much to say and too much to think about, and being spread way too thin to having an abundance of time and space to focus on myself. I didn't know where to direct all the energy I'd been pouring into teaching. I felt entirely unmoored.

Don't get me wrong here: it's bloody lovely not to go to work for a bit. And I was exceptionally fortunate that Rob was not only able, but so willing to help me do that while I tried to get well again. If you're going to be crippled with cramps and pooing yourself half the lifelong day, then it's nice to at least be able to do that at home with a hot water bottle and unlimited Bravo to watch on telly rather than wonder what the boys' nickname for you will be if you shit yourself in the middle of assembly. For the first couple of years we were together, I was the breadwinner (going into teaching around the time Rob decided to try to make it as a comedian), and this stint where my support was economical not just emotional has really stood me in good stead: never more so than the morning Rob found me crying in the shower trying to get ready for work, having downed half the contents of a pharmacy to make it in, and him saying so calmly, 'Why don't you just stop for a bit? We can manage on what I make for a while.' Knowing that someone has your back like that, no questions asked, meant more than the financial support itself.

Ulcerative colitis is a tricksy mistress and you just never know when she's going to rear her ugly head and mess with your life. Like all women, she reserves the right to change her mind at any point for no explicable reason, and what works to calm a flare one month just doesn't work the next. I've been on steroids, anti-inflammatories, immunosuppressants – the works; if big pharma makes it, then I've probably tried it. Because of the unpredictability of my ulcerative colitis, we made the decision to try to start a family very soon after we got married in case we ran into problems or I had another flare, because who knows how long it could last next time or what kind of interventions I might need. I became maniacally obsessed with trying to get pregnant as soon as possible.

At the time, you needed to have tried unsuccessfully for a year before the NHS would offer any help. I'd been told that because of the holy trinity of polycystic ovary syndrome (PCOS), endometriosis and ulcerative colitis I have going on, it might be tricky to get and then stay pregnant. I hadn't had a period for over a year and was in between intermittent colitis flares, so, I mean, it was an ideal time to try to bang out a baby right? Rob was excited to be a dad, but I think, if he's really truthful, he could have waited a little while longer, but I had this need, an actual visceral need, to start trying as soon as we could.

In fairness, Rob was very up for the trying too. The consultants had told us that because I wasn't having periods, there was no way of knowing if I was having any fertile windows, so the best way to approach trying would be to 'just' – *big* emphasis on that 'just' – have sex every other day, for all the days, until we hit the year mark and would qualify for help. For what I'm going to assume are obvious reasons, this part of the process excited Rob more than me. Imagine his crushing disappointment when we got pregnant within a week. Yes, it was a magical moment, discovering you're about to have a child, but I've never quite shaken the sense that he feels slightly cheated of his year of unfettered bonking. I, too, was obviously devastated ...

Which brings us to the part where we became parents – arguably the biggest impact anything has had on us, financially, emotionally, socially, physically and professionally.

Shifting Dynamics

Becoming parents tipped the scales for both of us in counterbalanced ways; I can imagine that if you're reading this, are already parents and, you know, have a pulse, it likely has for you too. For me, I took a step back from teaching to focus on being a mum and staying healthy, which has stalled my career path just a little to say the least; whereas becoming a parent has been massively important in Rob's career as, without it (and a worldwide panny-d), he wouldn't have started the podcast with friend and fellow comedian Josh Widdicombe. Without which I'd definitely not be writing this book. Though I've sometimes been given a 'right of reply' in the odd podcast episode or page of their book, *Parenting Hell*, this book means it is my turn – and Rob can have his 'right of reply' at the end too.

Like many, I struggled when I became a mum. I don't feel any shame in saying that, or at least I don't anymore. Because I did. I felt for a long time that I was doing something wrong, or not doing enough, somehow ungrateful for what I had. I struggled in a myriad of ways. In the early months and years, there were the classic struggles that all new parents face: the sleep deprivation, the 2am poo explosions, working out where to put all the thousand and one things your new baby needs. What I didn't expect were the unseen struggles – the silent assassins that people hadn't really mentioned before: just how much your identity changes, how different your life looks now and how insurmountable some of those challenges can feel. The person you've been for your entire life up until that baby pops out of you suddenly isn't really there anymore, and that's a hell of a plot twist to reconcile.

I hadn't really thought about the implications of becoming a mum beyond having a baby, but those new roles of 'Mum and Dad' (or 'Mum and Mum', and so on – remember to adapt what I'm saying to your own circumstances) change you and your partnership forever. You might have been the best husband and wife the world's ever seen, nary an argument or rolled eye betwixt you, but that dynamic is unspeakably different to the one you have as partners once you're parents. It's easy to be selfless and easy-going when it's just the two of you, but throw a small tyrant into the mix and, suddenly, free time and energy is as precious as water in an apocalypse.

From the point you become noticeably pregnant, that's the first, and sometimes only, thing people ask about. Even now, I have to remind myself to ask my friends about themselves not just their children, because having children is so all-consuming that it's easy to lose the person behind the parent. A lot of that is probably the physicality of becoming a parent, especially as the mum – on the whole, biologically speaking, the overwhelming bulk of growing, birthing and feeding a child falls on the mum. It's impossible to escape the (outrageously unfair) physical demands of having a child that fall on you if you're the mum.

You grow the baby, which is nine interminably long months of physical change and impact upon your body. Your body is no longer entirely your own; pregnancy changes what you can eat, what you can drink and what you can safely do. You might feel, or be being, sick for months on end. You're breathless because your body's pumping an average of 50 per cent increased plasma as well as an extra 18 per cent red blood cells around your ever-expanding body.[4] You gain weight, none of your clothes fit and you're not sure they ever will again. After nine months of the hardest physical work you'll probably ever do, what's your reward? Getting to go through hours and hours of physical pain and exertion to expel this baby from your body. Or, if you're not pushing it out, then having to undergo major abdominal surgery that has a weeks-long recovery time. Whichever exit your baby used, it takes a hell of a toll on your body and, instead of being sent to a nice spa in the Swiss Alps to recover, you're dispatched off home to look after an impossibly small baby who largely resembles a potato and needs feeding or changing or winding or rocking at what feels like 37-second intervals. If you're breastfeeding or attempting to – because breastfeeding is a whole other mountain of physical and emotional work – then the physical burden of keeping that baby alive and growing continues to fall on you. Yes, you and your partner are both sleep-deprived, but there is absolutely no way to even up the race of physical tiredness and, if I'm honest, I don't think there ever will be. No amount of 'Oh, I'll change their nappy' or 'You stay in bed – I'll take them downstairs' is ever going to remedy the fact that your body physically grew, birthed and sustained a whole human being.

Short of some major scientific advances, there's not much that can be done to even up the physical imbalance of the initial stages of becoming a parent. However, this sets the tone for the other stages to come. That physical disadvantage that mums are at right from the off is so hard to counter moving forward because the precedent has been set: Mum is the default for the baby and Dad's there to help where he can. How many times have you heard a dad say, 'Oh, they just want you' or 'They're probably hungry' two minutes after they've been fed, or perhaps the biggest cop-out of them all: 'You're just better at it than me; they recognise you from the womb'? Which might all be true; however, do you know how they'll recognise and take comfort from Dad? How Dad will get better at settling the baby? Time, familiarity and practice – none of which can happen if the baby's constantly being passed back to Mum with only the most cursory of attempts to 'help'. It's very much not rocket science. Practice makes perfect.

Being a good parent and being a good partner are two very distinct things, and they overlap massively. However, just because someone's one, it doesn't necessarily mean they're going to be the other, or be able to do both well. Fat lot of good knowing that becoming a dad made your husband a rubbish partner once the kids are here, I know, but short of shutting the uterus door once the tadpoles have bolted, what can you do if you suddenly find yourself as the default parent with no idea how to get back to yourself, or even work out who you are now – especially if your partner seemed to magically morph from a fairly modern man to a dad from the fifties once the baby was here? I would have divorced Rob a long time ago if he'd tried to pull that time-travelling stunt, but I never cease to be amazed by the number of friends I've spoken to who are surprised by how much Rob does as their partner 'would never': 'would never' go on a school trip or 'would never' take the children for their jabs. Rob has more than once said, 'but I do so much more than so and so …', and yes, that's true, but I also wouldn't have married or stayed married to someone who used the fifties' opt out of fatherhood option. I can count on one hand the number of times Rob's come home from work to a home-cooked meal on the table. It's very much not the fifties in our house. I have never once professed to be a domestic goddess, and popping some babies out of my lady parts certainly hasn't persuaded me that now is the time to go retro. Making allowances for our different work schedules aside (Rob's very full versus mine tumbleweed empty for many years), I have expected Rob to be as involved and present in the girls' lives as I am. I think every default parent out there has at some point muttered at least once (a day?!): 'They are *your* children too.'

What Does Default Parenting Mean Anyway?

Default parenting sounds quite fancy, but it's just the phrase that came to mind one night in the pub with a fellow mum friend when we were trying to articulate that feeling of always being in charge and trying not to just slag off our respective husbands. Honestly, I'm not sure if it's a proper phrase or whether I've unwittingly pinched it off someone or something I've read somewhere, but it encapsulated exactly what I was trying to express to my friend after perhaps slightly too much red wine. That pervasive feeling of always having to be on top of things. Of having to know what's going on. Of what's coming next and what's needed. Perpetually being the first line of defence for the family. It's the permanent assumption that you are always in charge, whether that be in the big physical ways of being at home to look after the children, or the not smaller but perhaps less in your face, more mental load ways of being across what everyone needs all the time. It's not just doing the jobs – that's almost the easy bit as tasks are finite. It's the anticipating, the planning, the arranging, the remembering, the monitoring, the deciding, the perpetual and infinite expectation of knowing everything all the time – that's the hard bit.

The reality is, I struggled when I first became a mum and I'm still struggling with some aspects of parenthood now, and I suspect I always will as things evolve. As Maria said in *The Sound of Music,* 'when the Lord closes a door, somewhere he opens a window'. When you just about get your head around one nonsensical thing about parenthood, there's another thing to spiral about just around the corner. With this in mind, I'm not here to offer advice – Jack Grealish* knows I haven't done it all right and I'm definitely still not doing it all right. What I am going to try to do, however, is work through the various stages of raising children and how the issues and problems of being the default show up, sometimes expectedly, but, mostly unexpectedly.

From better defining what it means to be 'the default parent' and exploring the daily expectations of your new role to the demands of looking after little ones and reflecting on the changes in your friendships and your relationship with your partner since becoming parents, we're going to work through the stages of childhood many parents experience. I'm going to offer some of the ways I've attempted to deal with the new and unique challenges each age and stage put in our way and (somewhat selfishly) cathartically release all the frustrations and rants I've had over the last 10 years of raising our girls.

Above all, I hope this book will help you feel seen, understood and less alone. Solidarity to the defaults, if nothing else.

* Insert deity of own choosing; personally, I pick Jack Grealish, but to each their own.

1

THE PARENT TRAP

(And Not the Fun One with Lindsay Lohan)

If you've been pregnant before or you're pregnant now, think about how many times someone asked you about your birth plan; how you've coped with pregnancy; whether you know what you're having; whether you're worried about labour or not – all really valid and pertinent questions, absolutely. The first time you get pregnant or go through labour is a huge thing to process, mentally and physically. Your body is going through something you have no frame of reference for, and you shouldn't underestimate it. Just because, as people will love to tell you, women have been making and birthing babies since we lived in caves, that doesn't make it any easier for you. *You* have not been birthing babies since you were in a cave. You have (probably) never lived in a cave, and what those semi-mythical ladies of times gone by managed to do without pain relief is immaterial. Do you know what else they used to do in the olden days? Die in childbirth. Do you know what else they did when they were in pain? Crushed up poppies and got out of their heads on opiates. This is the first time you're going to have physically pushed a child out of yourself and then be expected to keep it alive, so grant yourself a tiny bit of grace and don't get hung up on what people used to be able to do.

The only person you should be concerned about during the giving birth process is yourself – there are no medals for doing it without drugs or extra mum points for saying you actually quite enjoy labour. It's OK to be scared witless, it's probably psychologically more stable to expect pain relief for, you know, *pain*, and it's absolutely rational to say that the intense, drawn-out, extreme pain you went through before, during and after giving birth was not a pleasant experience, even if the end result was something lovely.

Giving Birth and Getting the Good Drugs

My two births were very different to one another. With my first, I had done the obligatory antenatal classes (more on paying for friends later on) and I thought I was armed with all the information and facts I needed to navigate giving birth successfully. Just to preface this, I so appreciated those classes I took: both the friends I made and the well-meaningness of the lady who ran the group were invaluable. However, it does feel like everyone you come into contact with in the lead up to giving birth has an agenda of sorts. The leader we had appeared to me to be so anti being induced that I left one session absolutely terrified of the ramifications, which, as it turned out once I'd looked into it myself, appeared to be a slightly increased chance of having a C-section.

If we're realistic, the messaging from almost all sources relating to birth and breastfeeding comes with some kind of agenda. I wish I'd taken a wider view of different opinions about the 'best' way to do things as I very much got stuck in a tunnel vision of the 'right' way to give birth, and the absolute necessity of breastfeeding.

Even in hospitals with medical professionals, it felt like there was a specific agenda. If you're trying to go against the grain and get yourself the good drugs or a C-section, you have to be vociferously vocal. Think about most of the people you've spoken to about labour – it all too easily starts to feel like a competition you don't actually remember entering about who 'managed' to have a natural birth, who took the 'easy' option, who endured the most pain or who had the most 'worthy' birth.

Who was in the most pain is almost worn as a badge of honour, which is ridiculous when you think about it. We shouldn't have had to be in pain for it to be a worthy birth. What is a worthy birth anyway?! Birth, however you do it, is a trauma on your body and surely we should be celebrating anything that can make it easier for women. We've spent decades fighting for a woman's right to choose her own direction in all the pathways of our lives. But yet it really does seem that some people just *have* to shout about how natural and un-medicated their births were or how beautiful the pain was. Which is ludicrous because when you step away and look at it sensibly, no matter what route you've taken – drugs, C-section, epidural, home birth or hospital – all being well, you all end up with a little baby at the end of it. There's quite literally no prize for doing it the hard way.

I totally understand that an uncomplicated vaginal birth is theoretically easier to recover from than a C-section or an epidural birth and you can leave hospital a lot faster afterwards. If that's what you choose to do, after being offered all the options, then more power to you my friend – to each their own. However, and this is a big however, vasectomies would also be a quicker recovery if you didn't give pain relief because men could drive themselves straight home afterwards without waiting for the effects to wear off. Just because something is better by one singular metric, it doesn't mean it's universally right for all people, and you have to take everything on balance. Epidurals are much less prevalent here than in the USA, for example, where around 47 per cent of women have an epidural during labour, compared to around 22 per cent in the UK, despite being free at the point of access. I didn't know this about epidurals when I had one, but they're actually associated with a reduction in maternal morbidity of about 35 per cent, probably because of the speed with which they can escalate interventions in an emergency without having to stop and anaesthetise.[1] So, by no means is it necessarily a bad thing to have one if you want to. It should be our choice, and that's the fundamental thing here: we need to be allowed to make the choice that's right for us and feel empowered by that choice without worrying what people think.

When I gave birth to my eldest daughter, I had a rough idea of what I wanted, and maybe I should have been less ambivalent about the treatment pathway I'd chosen. My premise was simple: as few interventions as possible, but absolutely anything necessary for the health of the baby or myself, with the caveat that I could and probably would change my mind about pain relief or interventions further down the line if I felt it necessary. I wasn't particularly keen on forceps or ventouse, but, ultimately, I would have anything if a doctor thought it necessary. To put it into context, I'm not a big hospital girly, but I have my fair share of health experience. Without getting too graphic, I've had a camera fully up inside my bowels pretty much twice a year since 2007, once without any sedation at all because I was still attempting to breastfeed (more on that attempt later). I've had debilitating cramps for days on end when my body couldn't keep anything inside itself and I'd end up losing enough blood I'd become anaemic. All alongside whole-body inflammatory flares during my worst episodes or severe reactions to my medications, both of which have needed hospital treatment to manage. None of this is to garner sympathy – it is what it is and a lot of people have it a lot worse; it's to explain that I understand pain, and I've got a pretty good pain threshold. So, imagine being told, given all of the above, upon my admission into the labour ward, that I 'don't have a proper frame of reference for pain' and therefore I didn't really understand that I wasn't actually in *that much pain*.

Advocating for yourself

To be told as a fully-grown woman, in literal labour, that you don't understand the pain you're in is spectacularly infantilising. Regardless of whether they thought I was being a big old baby or not, if someone says they are in pain and asks for help, then that's the end of it surely? How are you meant to advocate for yourself when the people in charge of your care are dismissive of the information you're giving them? How are you meant to feel confident in telling them how you're feeling when you have done that already and it felt like it didn't matter at all? You're so out of control of your body and what's happening to it at that moment, the last thing you need is to feel dismissed or ignored. I was all over the place at this point – I'd been throwing up for the best part of the day as my body's general response to cramping is to empty itself completely and, because of that, I had to go straight to the labour ward on a little hydration IV drip.

I was very spaced out in between contractions and wasn't really communicating effectively. However, I remember distinctly asking for pain relief a number of times, including an epidural, but being told that 'we weren't there yet'. I'm not sure where on the journey of preventable pain you have to be to get pain relief, but we most definitely were there. I was told it would be hours yet and to 'save' the drugs for later on.

I can only assume that my body responded out of pure spite at that point and progressed alarmingly quickly through the stages of labour, so I started pushing before any midwives made it back into the room. My daughter, who's obviously inherited her mother's pettiness, decided to poo in the womb just to panic everyone who'd been telling me to calm down for the last hour. With absolutely no medical training whatsoever, I have since managed to convince myself that, actually, if I had been given the drugs I was asking for, and some of the pain and therefore panic had been alleviated, I would have had a smoother and slower labour that actually would have been better for me and my body. Almost as if I, as a fully-grown adult, was capable of knowing my own body and, dare I say it, perhaps even knew my body better than those telling me no? Just perhaps though.

I don't want to be dismissive of medical professionals at all – there's absolutely no doubt that they've immeasurably improved the quality of my life, and perhaps even saved it before, and I wouldn't like to have been anywhere other than hospital for the births of my daughters, but that experience stayed with me.

Nothing terrible happened, but I couldn't in good conscience describe it as positive or empowering. You should be able to go into a brand-new and admittedly terrifying experience confident that you're going to be listened to and your decisions respected. You shouldn't have to have one 'bad' birth in order to get a good one afterwards.

Because I did get a good birth afterwards, I can't sing the praises of the labour ward at the Princess Royal University Hospital in Locksbottom highly enough. Maybe it's because I was a second-time mum so they gave what I was saying more credence, because this time I did in fact have a 'frame of reference' for the pain. Maybe it's because I went what I can only describe as bat-shit at the poor triage nurse in the labour and delivery ward. I wasn't communicating acceptably at all, just kind of screaming that I wouldn't go home even if I wasn't dilated enough, that I would just sit in Costa downstairs in reception and scare everyone with my wailing. For someone who is almost always ruthlessly polite to the point I have answered to names that aren't mine or eaten food I haven't ordered because I don't like to correct people, I was the rudest I've ever been.

I was reassured that they would find the anaesthetist to do an epidural as soon as they came out of the C-section that they were doing and I was admitted to the labour ward even though I didn't quite meet their 4cm dilated criteria because they listened to the fact that it moved so quickly last time. I didn't realise how anxious I had been about giving birth the second time around until I felt the fog of panic lift in that little curtained cubicle as I realised they were actually listening and acting on what I was telling them.

I've never done heroin, but when the epidural went in and started working, that's the closest thing I can imagine it's like. Pure and utter bliss. It's impossible to describe the feeling of labour – I've done it twice and I'm not sure I can adequately convey just how all-encompassing that feeling is. It's like nothing I've experienced before. We've all seen the little Instagram videos where they strap TENS machines to boys and turn it up to a level 10 and they collapse like those little toys that you push the underneath of, but I don't think that comes close. Contractions are a whole-body experience and, even in those blessed moments when you can feel one contraction abating, you know another is coming behind it, for hours and hours and hours. I'm not saying everyone should have an epidural; you do what feels right for you. I've got a friend who's got four children and says she almost enjoys labour, and, you know what, if that works for her then I'm pleased, and I would never dream of telling her she 'should' have something ...

I'm just saying that we are in 2026. There's no reason for you to be in excessive pain if you don't have or want to be. Don't be afraid to challenge what you're being advised. Just because most people do it one way, if that's not right for you then it doesn't matter how many un-medicated births your sister's friend's cousin Sandra has had. Maybe Sandra is a masochist who enjoys pain and showing off? Let Sandra crack on. If having pain relief or an epidural in your birth plan is going to alleviate some stress at a time when you could definitely do with relieving some, then don't be afraid to hold your ground on that.

Life Looks a *Little* Bit Different Now ...

Whether you meticulously plan for months or find yourself with a bonus babe on the way, I'd argue that there's little to no way to prepare yourself properly for what's coming round the corner of life at you. So why do we all do it? If it's such a massive, life-altering change, why do so many of us think, 'Yo ho ho, that's the life for me'? If we're being honest, really brutally, 'let's hope our children never read this and think we actually felt this way once we regained our sanity' honest, by every logical and tangible measure, your life gets 'worse' after having a baby. And it's very hard to find any evidence or anecdotes from parents who are saying the opposite.

Your social life is inevitably going to take a hit. Even if you weren't raving it up until the small hours round the Med on a playboy's yacht before kids, just leaving the house and going for dinner requires planning, packing and thought. Even then, even with a military operation level of preparation, you're still almost definitely going to have to change where your first choice of restaurant would be because all your decisions are now run through the parent gauntlet of 'If they scream blue murder for no discernible reason, how annoyed will the other diners be?' or 'How late can we push dinner before they are overtired, irrational banshees?'

That equation can apply to any aspect of your pre-baby life. In life before baby, you could leave the house with just a small bag, or nothing apart from your phone and a dream. You could make plans without having to factor in a hundred different variables. Your pay cheque was almost entirely your own to decide where it went, and what on. Any cash left over once your necessities were met was disposable – oh, the possibilities!

Life post-baby? You've got expenses coming out of your eyeballs. Everyone said having babies was expensive, but it's incomprehensible just how much of your money is now spent in Boots or on Amazon Prime. I think I'm single-handedly responsible for the expansion of Amazon in the mid-2010s. The middle-of-the-night panic-buying got entirely out of control – anything that seemed like it might make my life easier at 2am on three minutes' sleep got unceremoniously popped in my basket. And, if I'm honest, it never did make things easier. That tummy time mat thing I bought because our eldest liked it for three minutes at someone else's house? Screamed like she was being murdered when I put her on it at our house. The only thing that I could have spent money on at that point which would have helped would have been a night nanny. However, even then, I would have been too addled to actually, you know, sleep. Because every single second I watched the baby to make sure she was still alive. Despite having not come anywhere close to accidentally killing someone in the first 29 years of my life, I became convinced that I was somehow going to accidentally manage it now. Rationality? Sanity? Reason? Poof! Gone! All disappeared the moment she popped out of me.

Breastfeeding: A Blessing or a Curse?

The seeds of being the default are sown early on in the dynamics of having a baby. As a mum, your body theoretically has the ability to solely feed and sustain a baby for the first six months of their life without any outside contributions. That's a hell of a responsibility for someone whose body has already been through the biggest physical marathon of being pregnant and giving birth, and that responsibility is absolutely overwhelming.

Big, *big* caveat here: lots of people struggle with breastfeeding, so just because our bodies are technically able to do it, it doesn't necessarily mean we can or should do it if it's not right for us as individuals. For all our sakes, we need to normalise the mum not being the only one responsible for feeding the baby, whether that's from choice or necessity. I struggled massively with breastfeeding my first and the obsession with 'breast is best' almost tipped me over the edge physically and mentally. Yes, it is best, no one disputes that. Formula, however, is also perfectly fine if it means your baby gets fed and your mental and physical health isn't being slowly driven off a cliff. You can, of course, pump too if you want to stick exclusively to breast milk. I tried that for the first three months after our eldest was born because she wouldn't latch. I know it works for some people, but I really struggled with it. I never managed to get more than one feed ahead and it felt like I spent most of the day (and night) hooked up to that cursed machine. The whooshing sound of the pump will haunt my dreams until the day I pop my clogs. *However*, in what will become a running theme of this book, DO WHAT WORKS FOR YOU and don't worry about what anyone else is doing, or thinks, or is saying. It doesn't matter what did or didn't work for me – that was my experience, and other people's experiences will be totally different. The main thing here is to find a way to share the load, by whatever means works for you and you're happy with.

There's something very democratic about a bottle of milk, whether formula or expressed. There's absolutely nothing about that bottle that I can do better than you – so have at it Daddy, I'm going back to sleep. If you don't want to introduce a bottle, there is always something your partner can do. I'm going to repeat that again – listen up non-defaults too: *there is always something you can do*. If you can't breastfeed, then fine, I won't hold it against you, though I definitely did hold it against Rob as it's very hard not to feel resentful at 2am when you're the one with boobs, to be honest. But there is always something you can be doing. Could you fetch your partner a drink? A snack? Could you change the baby's nappy? Could you go in the other room with the baby once they're fed and resettle them?

That biological responsibility is both the biggest blessing and, if I'm honest, a bit of a curse I think. While I loved the fact that I could breastfeed my second and felt very validated by being able to do so, when you're the one solely responsible for feeding them and the only one able to, the time you can spend away from your baby is limited to how long they can go without having milk, which, at the beginning, are impossibly short windows of time – time in which there are always 103,841 things more important to do than remember who you are it feels.

This isn't to say that there aren't people who love breastfeeding and want it to continue for years and years. I wouldn't change the experience of breastfeeding my second daughter for the world. However, that came off the back of a very difficult experience with my first, where I felt exceptionally pressured to continue in what was an ultimately futile quest for her to have only breast milk, even though I was clearly struggling mentally and physically.

It's a personal choice. If it's important to you and you love it, then more power to you. If you're happy to be the first line of feeding defence, then that's brilliant and I fully support you making that choice if it's right for you. Everyone's set-up is different and, after feeling so judged for even thinking about giving my eldest formula when we were struggling, I would never judge any parent for any of the choices they make if they're right for them.

So, of course, it's not that I think the choice to breastfeed is problematic, it's the fact that it's so easy to establish a precedent where Mum is first and foremost the responsible parent. This then bleeds almost imperceptibly into not just feeding but general baby-looking-after. When those babies popped out of me I didn't magically become the master of baby settling or the psychic interpreter of baby needs, it was practice. Just because I have the milk, it doesn't mean I'm the sole provider of all that baby's needs. Don't let biology get in the way of meeting each other as much as you can in the middle, however that works for you.

The Overwhelm

Obviously, having a little tiny mate with you at all times is a lovely thing. However, it's also overwhelming. If you're having one of those mornings or, let's be honest, afternoons, evenings or nights, where it's all just too much, no one's slept, the coffee's run out, they've had three poo explosions and are on their seventh outfit of the day, and when you eventually manage to leave the house with your nappy bag, spare outfits, extra layers, milk, dummies and teething toy while looking suspiciously like Worzel Gummidge because, of course, there was no time for you to get ready, it can feel really overwhelming and relentless. The universe likes to keep us humble, so, remember, even a good day can turn and, of course, a difficult day can always, *always* get more difficult. There will be the days when your precious little babe won't sleep in their pram on your walk, screams loud enough to make your ears bleed in that lovely little café you've been fantasising all night about, won't sit in a high chair so you can eat the first hot thing you've had all day and probably kicks your now-cold coffee over you and you walk home on the verge of tears wondering why you even bothered trying to leave the house in the first place. Those days are the days when just being able to leave the house without anyone or anything else seems like a distant fever dream.

It's also massively overstimulating being a new mum – the noise, the physical touch of a baby on you, the carousel of things you constantly need to do – and sometimes just a walk by yourself is all you need to reset your head, however briefly. Rob forced me to walk to the Co-op by myself when our youngest was maybe 2 or 3 weeks old as he could obviously sense an impending implosion. I was utterly overwhelmed at that point and, while I was reluctant to leave her even for half an hour to walk to the shops, that chilly little walk where I wasn't checking her temperature, worrying if she'd wake up when I stopped walking, worrying when she'd last been fed, worrying about letting go of the pram and letting her roll in the road, convincing myself someone would pinch her out of the pram if I looked at the stuff in the shop for too long instead of looking at her every two and a half seconds, really did help.

Reading that back, I don't think I appreciated at the time just how heightened everything is with a newborn, because those anxieties are insane when you list them out. I have never once let a pram roll in the road. Or left her unattended in a shop for someone to pinch. The postpartum brain gymnastics are wild. Probably a combination of raging hormones and extreme exhaustion, but it's very hard to remember you're a rational adult at that point. I've digressed quite wildly off the point I was trying to make here – maybe my brain's not bounced back quite the way I thought it had, but that's a problem to worry about for another day. The point was that, once you're a parent, you can't leave the house alone unless you arrange for someone else to have the kids, and that is hugely overwhelming, so finding anything that can ease that overwhelm occasionally, even if it's a 10-minute solo walk to the newsagent, is so important.

The Guilt

We've evolved way past only having one way to physically keep our babies alive – there's absolutely no reason why it always has to be Mum anymore, but trying to tell the irrational part of yourself that is really hard in the early days. That ever-present little whisper in your brain asking, 'Shouldn't I be with them?' is so hard to quell. Even when they're with their other parent, who is equally qualified and capable of having them, that little insidious whisper that you're somehow being a bad mum, a neglectful parent, a selfish person is really pervasive.

I had to get my mum to babysit while I went to hospital a few weeks after I'd given birth because they were worried about how much I was still bleeding, and it felt weirdly like such a treat and also such a waste. I'd pumped two bottles of milk and had a precious couple of hours to myself and I spent it in Lewisham hospital with a doctor and some student nurses looking up my bits, which, if I'm honest, is not my idea of a good time. I also felt extremely guilty at leaving the baby 'by herself' even though she wasn't 'by herself', she just wasn't with me. She was actually with my mum who is an amazing mum – and a paediatric nurse to boot. I mean, if you're leaving your baby with anyone, then someone who's raised three girls and is an ex-Great Ormond Street nurse is not a bad shout. I think some of it is very old-school evolutionary biology, because the rational part of my brain knows that my baby couldn't be left in a better place and will be absolutely fine while I'm not there. But the cavewoman wiring in my evolutionary make-up is telling me that if I wasn't with my baby then she'd starve, get eaten by wild dogs or thrown out of the cave as a waste of resources.

A lot of that insane mum-guilt thinking was reinforced by the fact that every time I wanted to do something without the baby, I had to effectively ask someone. I had to check what Rob was doing and whether he could have her, or I had to phone grandparents and arrange for them to come over. I had to impinge on other people's lives and, even though they were happy to help me, and beyond happy to spend time with the baby, I still felt like I was imposing. That feeling was hard enough to shake when it was for something very necessary like making sure I wasn't about to waste away from leaking my body's blood supply out of my hoo hah, but even harder to rationalise when it was for something that didn't feel 'important', like self-care or socialising.

Of course, there aren't many ways of getting around the fact that the pregnancy and birth bit of parenting comes down to the parent who's carrying the child – that's just the deeply unfair and outrageously inconvenient reality. However, once that baby is earth-side, it's fair game. A baby's got two parents and two parents can share that load.

Having a Parenting Plan

You might have heard the saying, 'If you want to make God laugh, then make plans.' Good news – you've birthed a tiny little deity of your very own! Babies are famously not the most reasonable or rational beings because they're, well, babies and they don't know, understand or care about all your careful planning. We all make a birth plan, which often goes entirely out the window anyways, but what about a parenting plan? That's when the shit really hits the fan.

A lot of pre-baby conversations are very practical because they have to be. Having a discussion about what kind of maternity and paternity leave you'll both take is pretty fundamental at this point because, obviously, someone has to be at home with the baby all day and you need to keep a roof over everyone's heads, but what about the nuts and bolts of the day-to-day of your lives?

Once the decision had been made that I wasn't going to go back to work immediately, what should have happened, in hindsight, was a whole raft of follow-up conversations about what that would mean practically for us. We'd decided that Rob would focus on his career and I would take a break from mine, and that worked well for us both from a practical standpoint and also for my health. What we didn't discuss was all the ramifications of that decision and what it would look like in reality.

Deciding that your partner will stay in work full time, that you'll take maternity leave and go back maybe part time in a year leaves a lot of grey area. And do you know what thrives in the grey? Default parenting. 'Taking maternity leave' or 'Staying at home to look after the baby' might sound simple enough, but they cover a lot of sins and you're going to be on the hook for them if you do not establish those boundaries early doors.

It's never too late to have a conversation about your roles and epectations for the other parent: who's going to be responsible for what at home? How are you splitting your time when one of you isn't at work? However, the stakes feel so much higher once the baby's here. While I'll never admit to being irrationally tired and perpetually furious post the birth of our eldest, I will say that I think I would have had a much more productive conversation about who was meant to be doing what before she arrived than afterwards, when I was so tired and hormonal that I absolutely was not rational for months. Rob would probably argue that I'm still not, but, for once, he doesn't get a say. Yes, you're going to end up doing a lot together, especially in the early days when you're learning how you're meant to keep this tiny human alive, but if you're both doing everything then no one's ever getting a break. And you will need a break, even if it's just a walk to Sainsbury's, to reset and BREATHE.

Don't get me wrong, I'm not saying you should be keeping a spreadsheet of exactly who does what (and I do know a couple who kept a spreadsheet and, believe me when I say, that way madness lies), but as someone who has only realised a lot of this once I was already in it, it's a lot easier to lay out a rough plan of what both your lives are going to look like post-baby when you're still pre-baby.

But if you're stuck in the depths of this at the moment and aren't sure how to navigate yourself back out, then the below might be useful as a starting point. Identify who's doing what and ask yourselves why. Is there a logical reason why you're doing it? If not, then how could you divide this to work better for you both? You can revisit this as often as works for you.

1. **Childcare admin (if applicable).** Who is doing nursery drop-off and pickup? Who is responsible for receiving and actioning letters/emails? What about packing their

bags in the morning? What's their key worker/childminder called? Who is booking parents' evening appointments? Do you have the number for the nursery office? What date's the nativity and have you booked it off work?

2. **Logistics.** Who is booking and taking them to their activities? Who's making them breakfast? What time is your alarm set for versus mine? What time is bedtime and how does that fit into our existing routines? Who's in charge of bath time?

3. **Seasonal.** Who is picking and buying presents, buying birthday cards, wrapping presents, inviting family and friends, organising the food? Who is responsible for booking seasonal activities like seeing Father Christmas and being aware of when those booking windows open?

4. **Life admin.** Who books their activities? Who checks the passports are in date? Who's registered them for child benefit or free childcare hours? Do their clothes still fit? What do we need to replace?

5. **Feeding.** Who's in charge of the following: Is there formula in the cupboard? Are the bottles clean? Have the dummies been sterilised? Do we have spares? Is there suitable food in the fridge? Can you make a balanced meal out of it? What is everyone eating? What do they like now? Do they have their healthy snacks for nursery?

6. **Appointments.** Which doctor are they registered with? Who's the primary contact? Are they up to date with their jabs? What about the dentist? When do they need to start going?

You don't need me to carry on, as we'll be 11 pages deep and not even close to the end of the tasks that need doing, but it's a starting point to open discussions at least. So, in whatever way works for you and your partner, and at whatever stage of parenting you're at, because it's *never* too late, start communicating about what you want and need to make the parenting journey work for *both* of you.

What I found helpful when trying to share the load with Rob was to start the discussion with a manageable quantity of tasks rather than try to deal with everything all at once, then build up. Establish the principle that it's labour to be divided and then work up from there. Or write your own list out on a massive scroll to be dramatically unfurled next time you're feeling self-righteously angry about how much you do. Up to you.

2

WHO AM I NOW?

(Life with a Newborn)

When you've spent nine months growing a child and then birthing it, I don't think there's a person in the land who doesn't think, 'Oh I deserve a nice little break from work now', and the majority of people wouldn't swap their maternity leave even if their partner offered to take up the mantle of full-time childcare responsibilities. Unless your baby is going almost straight into full-time childcare or you have a nanny ready to go as soon as they pop out, one of you is going to have to take a significant break from work to look after them.

Overwhelmingly, that falls on the parent who has given birth – and there's no getting around the impact that has on the parent stepping away from their career, temporarily or otherwise. I hadn't prepared myself for just how much of my identity was wrapped up in my work when I gave up teaching. When that identity wasn't there anymore, and was effectively replaced with a new identity as a 'default parent', I'm not ashamed to say I struggled to reconcile the new me with the old. I didn't know who I was or who I was meant to be.

Going Back to Work

When I got pregnant and went on 'maternity leave', I wasn't really on maternity leave. I didn't have a job to go back to and so I wasn't working to any timeline really. This made it much easier for me to slip into the role of the default parent as not only was Rob's career really taking off, but his work was out-earning mine. While it's obviously not all about financial gain, it just didn't make any practical sense for him to turn down work so I could go and earn a fraction of what he was while making myself poorly into the bargain.

I often wonder whether I would have gone back if I'd been officially off on maternity leave instead, as half the decision would have been made for me. I would have had a date to work towards and a familiar environment to return to with colleagues who I knew and loved. However, when we were approaching the year mark with our eldest, I was so befuddled by parenthood that the thought of trying to get my head back in the game and having to prove myself in an interview with people who didn't know what I was capable of pre-baby seemed insurmountable. So, I did what any sensible person would do when they feel overwhelmed, and promptly got pregnant with another baby and put the whole decision off for another day. Incidentally, it turns out it would be six more years before I attempted (key word: attempted) another interview – more on that later.

Jokes aside, obviously parents have to work. Ostensibly, parental leave is meant to be able to be split much more evenly now, to share the load of those really hard newborn days between both parents. And I've seen a few friends' husbands and partners enthusiastically take this option. By and large, however, I think we all know many more fathers fairly eagerly returning to work a few weeks after the birth of their progeny because, deep down, they know what all mums know: it's easier being at work than it is at home. Not because they lack a mother's biological superiority and innate maternal instincts to look after the baby, but because they get whole parcels of uninterrupted and 'guilt-free' time to live their life largely the way they did pre-baby but validated by the need to provide. (By the way, I'm not sure maternal instincts actually exist or maybe I just have a heart of stone – I think they're born of necessity. You're left with a baby and it needs looking after ... so you work it out and look after it.)

Work is a funny old concept. What do you do when you've spent years building a career you were proud of and you're suddenly catapulted into an entirely different life? You're still working, but you're not 'working'? The financial autonomy that comes with having a job, and the structure and validation work provides, has been replaced with spending 24 hours a day looking after a tiny irrational being who is quite literally always there and your partner still gets to leave the house to go to their own job every day.

But, when your partner gets home from work, you have to remember: You. Have. Been. Working. Too. I don't care if that work looked like drinking lukewarm coffee while the real housewives of Salt Lake City screamed 'receipts' at each other. What you've actually done in the day with a newborn is almost immaterial; you've been working too. If everyone in your house is alive, fed and clothed at the end of the day, then you have been working. You just haven't been paid for it and, admittedly, it looks a lot less like working because if I'd shown up to my old teaching job wearing pyjamas with baby sick in my hair they'd have probably sent me home.

The financial angle is one I've seen held over the heads of my friends. We've all heard it to some degree, whether it's been intimated by our partner or it's our friends trying to rationalise their partner's shitty behaviours – 'He can't take that time off because there's a big project and he won't be involved if he misses the start.' But women also lose those valuable months and years that could be spent building their career. How many men have gone part time after a baby versus how many women? We all know about the gender pay gap – in 2024, men out-earned women by 18 per cent[1] – but how much of that is because women lose momentum, even if that is just temporarily, when they have a baby? Of course, not all default parents are women – the career impact applies to whoever assumes that default role. It's an impossible circle to square, because, by and large, we want to be off with our babies but that doesn't mean we have to go quietly into the night and accept the inequalities that come with that, both at home and at work. We might not be able to level the playing field entirely, and perhaps we wouldn't even want to, but it could and should be a lot more evenly split than it is.

What probably didn't help at the start of our parenting journey was that Rob and I weren't on a traditional maternity/paternity leave schedule. Rob's self-employed and, to keep a roof over our heads and also keep momentum building in his career, he couldn't really say no to some of the work offers that were coming in. Sometimes you are just between a rock and a hard place and there's nothing to be done other than plough on through. He wasn't being sent down the mines or anything, but I'd argue that with a newborn baby at home and a wife on the edge of a mental breakdown because of the trials of breastfeeding, probably going to a little house in west London and trying to decipher challenges from Alex Horne for *Taskmaster* wasn't exactly what Rob needed. However, when he came home from filming, I can't express how little sympathy I had for him being covered in goose poo from rolling across a running track all morning (it made sense at the time I think). All he wanted was to lie down and go to sleep as he'd been at work all day. All I wanted was for him to take the baby so I could lie down and sleep because I'd been at work all day.

I'm really lucky (though this should be the norm) that I had a partner who very much saw me as equally important in our dynamic. Who recognised that he couldn't go off and do what he needed to do in his career without someone, me in this instance, being at home and keeping everything going. Financially, Rob has never once made me feel like our money is anything other than just that – ours, even though he's technically the one earning it. However, even though I knew that was how he felt, and there were years early on when I financially supported us, it was, and still is to an extent, a concerted effort not to get in my own head about not having my 'own' money. We're a partnership and I wouldn't expect either of us to make big purchases or important financial decisions unilaterally anyways, but the stakes really get raised up a notch when one of you technically isn't earning for however long, whether that's reduced hours, working part time to fit around childcare or longer periods of being a stay-at-home default parent and not 'working' at all.

I've worked and earned my own money since I was 16 and I wasn't used to relying so totally on someone else. It wasn't not being able to spend lots of money on something, because I didn't do that even when I was working, it was the knowing I could, *if* I wanted to. And I didn't have to technically answer to anyone but myself. Like so many other things since becoming a parent, the loss of my independent financial identity was a hard one to reconcile. It was something I hadn't really considered would impact the way I saw and thought of myself long term when we decided I'd take a step back from my career.

I, like many women, didn't want to go back full time after I had the girls – I wanted to really enjoy them as babies and toddlers. Also, from a very practical point of view, Rob doesn't work a nine-to-five, or Monday-to-Friday, job. His work can be any time of the day or night, any day of the week; sometimes he's out of the house for a few hours and sometimes he's touring for a few weeks, so the childcare we would have needed for me to return to work would have made it difficult to justify from a financial perspective.

There's not a day when I don't appreciate how lucky I was to be in that position of being able to choose to go back to work or not at that point. I could stay at home and enjoy my babies and not feel financially pressured to get back to a job that, though I loved it, I had also found very stressful. I never take for granted that a lot of people don't have the choices I had.

Your New Default Identity

When I stepped back from working, I didn't realise how much of me I was also stepping back from, and the void that it left. Of course, so much of that space was filled with our two delicious girls and all the satisfaction, hard work and enjoyment I got from spending time with them and raising them. However, a career isn't just how you fill your time. It's somewhere where your opinions are respected. Where you're achieving tangible things. Where you can use your experience and knowledge to achieve goals. Where you are your own person, independent of anyone else. You are you.

No one told me that, when I became a mum, my new identity would be the do-er of everything, forever. It's my job for now and all time to feed everyone three meals a day, know what's in the cupboards, make sure everyone has clean clothes and the right equipment, plan parties that the kids will enjoy, manage precarious friendships, make sure their reading is at the right level, buy presents for the hundreds of birthday parties they get invited to, make sure their shoes still fit, pack sun cream in the bags, take them to the dentist, and the list goes on and on. While I totally accept that my needs and wants come second to those of the girls (they're my children after all and I chose to have them – who else's responsibility would they be?), as default parents, we often find ourselves slipping down the family hierarchy because of the absence of paid work. Paid work is the key phrase there, because, as I've said, defaults are working, and I'd say working harder than anyone sitting in an office. You're probably working harder and for more hours than you've ever worked in your life, but because no one's given you a contract and a pay cheque it's like it doesn't register. Your work is done 24 hours a day, 7 days a week and it's almost so constant it's not noticed, which is maddeningly frustrating. If you had to leave to go to an office to parent every day, it would be infinitely more difficult to ignore. And double, triple, quadruple ... whatever comes after quadrupling ... that frustration for those parents who are the default and have *also* gone back to work! I had obviously taken an extended break from my career before we had the girls, but there are so many mums who do go back, in whatever capacity, who are still firmly in the default position even when the logic isn't logic-ing. Working mothers are almost twice as likely to turn down or delay a promotion because of family obligations, and more than double the number of mothers versus fathers have seriously considered leaving entirely or reducing their hours because of childcare issues.[2] Mothers, working or otherwise, are managing 71 per cent of household tasks compared to men, who manage 45 per cent.[3] The maths isn't mathing here gentlemen – there's absolutely no reason why this isn't more evenly split, *especially* for the households where you've both gone back to work.

Just how consuming my new default identity was really surprised me when I became a mum for the first time – I didn't realise how all-encompassing this new role would be. I know that sounds really naïve and selfish; what did I realistically think was going to happen? Obviously, I knew that having and raising a baby was an incredible amount of work, work I was excited and happy to do. However, I didn't prepare for the hit it my identity would take as a person, the way I saw myself and the way I felt about myself. At the same time as I was celebrating the addition of something new and incredible in my life, I was also mourning the loss of my old life and career, and those two things aren't mutually exclusive. It just means I'm human.

Your world can feel like it gets really small, really quickly when you have a baby. I thought I'd be adding 'mother' to my identity, another facet of the kaleidoscope of all the things and experiences that make me myself. However, what I wasn't expecting was just how totally I became almost entirely 'Mum'. Just how hard it was to carve out the physical time, emotional headspace or personal permission to work towards getting back to who I was before. I don't think you ever go back fully, and I wouldn't want to – those two girls are the most important things in my life, but it's a balance. I was a person for 29 years before them, and that person is important in this equation too. You're a better mum if you're also allowed to be a person. The hard part is finding the time to do that.

Clawing back the concept of self-care

The division of responsibility goes way beyond who's going back to work and who has physical responsibility for the baby during the working day. When are you seeing your friends? When are you getting in some self-care? When are you carving out time for your interests and hobbies that might not be work, but are an important part of helping you feel anchored to a version of yourself that can feel a million miles away once you've had a baby?

One of the things I was told a lot, and I mean *a lot*, is 'make sure you take time for yourself too'. Which is all well and good when it's coming from someone a decade in (and I'm all too painfully aware of the irony that it's taken me nigh-on 10 years to get enough headspace and time to actually sit and write this book), but for the new mum of a small screaming potato who needs feeding, changing, jiggling, cleaning and tummy-timing, where is this time of which you speak? How does one carve out these mystery minutes to have a shower or put on some make-up? You might have been the most beautifully well-put-together person in your life pre-baby. Remember when you had time to choose an outfit? Remember when your clothes weren't covered in mystery bodily fluids and dried melty puffs? When you had time to look like anything other than the pigeon lady in *Home Alone 2*? Well, congratulations, those days are behind you now.

I'm not saying they're never coming back – I've seen the unicorns on the school run; the ones whose outfits look cohesive, the women in the soft play who look like they glanced in a mirror before leaving the house, the ones wearing two matching shoes. How are they doing it? I don't know. I can only assume that there's some ritual satanic sacrifice going on here, because the kind of headspace and physical time to do that while being in charge of children is something that has eluded me for a long time. I have nice clothes. I know I do. The postman knows I do because he delivers the boxes here on an alarmingly regular basis. It's the time in the morning to choose an outfit, to shower, to blow-dry my hair and maybe, just maybe, put on some make-up that I don't have time for – or I can't make the time for. When you're also trying to get babies or small children up, fed, dressed, teeth cleaned and their bags packed with whichever Duke of Edinburgh-length list of things they need for that day, something's got to give, and what always seems to give is the time and personal space I need to make myself feel not like a crusty old foot.

I appreciate that self-care and time for you is ridiculously hard to factor in with a newborn when it feels like it's all hands on deck all the time, but trying to establish precedents with your partner early on makes it so much easier in the long run, even if it's just proactively planning for things that you will all do together with the baby at the weekend or in the evenings so that you know definitively that you'll have that load shared.

Trying to balance it all

Self-care and socialising in a post-baby world all have to be balanced against the needs of the baby and the family. Because, if you're the default, that child is with you unless you've explicitly arranged otherwise. Anything you want or need to do has to be weighed against arranging for someone else to look after them. There's a running ticker tape in my head now continually asking, *Is it worth it? Can you justify the time/expense against the needs of everyone else?*

Before children, I didn't have to justify how I spent my time or my money to anyone else. I could book whatever I wanted into my diary, spend what I wanted, or whatever I had, and there was no one I had to explain that to. The judgement on the choices I now have to make whenever I want to do anything, whether real or imagined, is overwhelming as a default parent.

Unless you're some insane landed gentry level of rich, you probably don't have a team of nannies, cleaners, childminders and staff to pick up the extra work that having children creates. Once you've had children, there's always something to consider. It gets massively easier once they start nursery or school. However, at the beginning, someone has to be with them. All. The. Time. And, if you're like me and your partner went pretty much straight back to work, then that person is you. In a lot of ways, this was amazing for me. I'm a very social person and I love my friends, but I also love my own company. Suddenly, having a delicious little baby to go on walks with, go to cafés with or push round the shopping centre was best of both worlds – I was essentially by myself but I had company. But it also sent me a bit loopy in the early days – still does if I'm honest. Because it never ends – there isn't a foreseeable end point when your responsibilities stop. Ever.

Rob is the nicest man I've ever met (tied with my dad) and we still struggled to balance what we each needed at that time. The competition between our careers, social lives, roles as Mum and Dad, and our relationship is something that's had to constantly evolve since becoming parents to navigate the new challenges thrown at us. I cannot imagine how much harder it would have been if I'd been with someone who didn't prioritise me and the girls in the way that he does. Ultimately, a baby is going to make things harder in a lot of ways, at least for a time, and if your partner is a bit of a selfish arse before having children then that's not going to change afterwards. If there's one thing women know, it's that men will generally do as little as they can get away with and probably want a congratulations for whatever it is they do manage, so advocate for yourself and your needs too. You cannot pour from an empty cup and all that jazz, so whatever self-care you can squeeze in, fill your cup. You deserve it.

Sleep Wars and How to Win Them

Sleep is a hugely tense issue once you've got children – and not just babies. At the time of writing, our youngest is 8 and we're back to getting up multiple times a night to get her back to sleep. Not once in the last 10 years since having our eldest could I genuinely say I've had enough sleep.

The default parent, as I think we all know, is disproportionately hit in the sleep stakes. Studies suggest that women lose around 40 minutes of sleep per night after having a baby, whereas men only lose 13 minutes on average.[4] (Given that most mums tend to be the defaults in their families, I think it's fair to extrapolate that out to defaults/non-defaults.) This isn't just in the baby stages when you could argue that, if you're breastfeeding, that disparity is much harder to even up – it seems to carry on well into parenthood. A lack of 'explicit negotiation' between partners means that women often take on the majority of caring for their children, physically and emotionally, not just during the day, but also into the night – 'subjugating their own needs' even when they've returned to employment.[5] So, it looks like the sleep disparity never quite evens up either in quality or quantity. Interesting. Worth remembering next time you're having a 'discussion' about tiredness with your partner. What that research also says to me is that we're not communicating properly with our partners. If that default responsibility for children is carrying on overnight when it isn't for our partner and also long after breastfeeding is over, then that's something we need to talk about. Default thrives in the grey; so don't let it be grey for a lack of 'explicit negotiation'.

Sleep is massively important for our physical and mental health, and the idea that you're less entitled to it because you're not technically going to work is ridiculous. You've probably heard the argument that your needs aren't as important as your partner's because you can be tired with a baby but they can't be tired at work. Let's just rewind that bit though: you've quite literally got the responsibility of keeping a tiny delicate human being alive, fed and happy. Sounds pretty important to me.

The clever clogs at the Division of Sleep Medicine at Harvard Medical School have tested our brain function and abilities after periods of sleep deprivation. Any prolonged wakeful periods beyond a 16-hour wake window – in other words, if you're not regularly getting somewhere close to 8 hours a night – leads to decreased brain activity. This leads to a lower level of alertness as well as a reduction in concentration, working memory, mathematical capacity and logical reasoning.[6]

It isn't just cognitive function that's impacted. Your mood will be too. It's hard, if not near impossible, to be a rational, empathic, good-decision-making person if you're addled with sleep deprivation. In a study of couples and the impact of poor sleep, they reported more conflict in their romantic relationships following poor nights of sleep.[7] It's an oxymoron of parenting that at the point when you need each other's support the most, you can feel the most at odds. For me and Rob, nothing induced more tension early on than the constant battle and festering resentments of who was working the hardest and who was the most tired.

It's not productive to constantly argue over who's the most tired, but it's also unspeakably galling to have your need for sleep minimised because you're not technically 'going to work'. You're responsible for the safety and well-being of your precious little dumpling and you're physically not going to be safe or be making good decisions if you're too tired to string a thought together, drive a car or keep your eyes open. So there it is. Science is on your side. You absolutely *are* the most tired and now you can prove it.

If you're the non-default, then there's adult conversation at work and colleagues who listen to what you're saying (hopefully); you have your own identity. You probably have a commute, where you can sit/stand/be wedged onto a tube/train/bus where you can listen to a podcast uninterrupted, read your book and drink a takeaway coffee that's still hot. You get a lunch break. You might pop into the pub on the way home. You might swing by the shops as you were passing. And you can do all of this as an individual person and still come home and think you're the most tired because you've been at work? Absolutely no thank you. I know all the good books and parenting experts say not to make it a competition, but sometimes you've got to say 'fuck that'. In the early days, it absolutely is and, to be honest, it was a competition I felt viscerally that I had to win. If nothing else had happened that day, I had to get Rob to agree that, yes, I was the most tired. I didn't even care if he actually thought that, I just needed him to validate my experience of being physically and mentally exhausted.

The Necessity of Finding Parent Friends

Your days are impossibly long as a new mum, probably not helped by the fact that you've been up half the night as well. Day and night fast become almost meaningless concepts with a newborn because you're probably going to be up for most of the time anyway. 'The days are long but the years are short' is what they say, which is great and everything, but really unhelpful when you're in the newborn trenches. My girls are older now and, while I totally understand how quickly the time goes in retrospect, mums with newborns aren't looking at it in retrospect with a pair of lovely rose-tinted glasses and treasuring those precious moments. They just want to get through the day feeling somewhat like they've got their shit together and not cry in a corner for their long-lost selves when they had the ability to leave the house without milk sick dribbled down their back.

Your new life with a newborn, while absolutely filled with joy, delicious little sniffs of their head and the sense of Zen you get when a tiny baby is asleep sprawled across your chest while you're watching some wealthy white women scream expletives at each other in Beverly Hills on the telly, can also feel really overwhelming and, to be honest, really bloody lonely. When the front door shuts and your partner leaves for work, those hours can loom very large, just stretching out interminably in front of you. I've got two sisters who I'm really close to and a big group of amazing friends, but, at the time, I was the only one of all those brilliant women to have had a baby and it felt quite isolating as I was no longer free when they were. I couldn't come and meet anyone for drinks at 7pm on a Friday after work because I'd be in the throes of trying to persuade my potato to go to sleep, and they couldn't come and watch me cry into a coffee at 9am on a Wednesday morning because they were at work.

So, I did what probably thousands upon thousands of people have done when they find out they're pregnant, and booked onto the ubiquitous antenatal classes in order to make friends. Sure, the information was going to be useful as well, but let's stop pretending we wanted to learn – what we were all there for was the network of people in our immediate area, all of whom were going to be blessed with their own screaming potatoes in the few weeks before and after you popped yours out. Whether you find those friends through private antenatal classes, classes at the hospital, or you just accost similarly bedraggled women in the park pushing a pram around, finding a group of people who are going through almost exactly what you are will keep you sane.

Filling the day as the default can feel really hard, and it's much less hard when there are five or six of you working as a team. Between us, we almost had one fully functioning brain in the throes of sleep deprivation; between us, we could pretty much work out when classes were meant to be on and how to get there; between us, we could generally be somewhere, fully dressed and with at least 70 per cent of the things we needed. It took the pressure off finding things to do, because whoever was feeling proactive that week would find something or somewhere to fill the morning. And we moved en masse; absolutely zero independent thoughts for the first six months. If someone was signing up for baby yoga, then we all were. If I was driving to the next town for baby sensory, then we all were. When one of us booked a ticket for the baby cinema at a picture house in Greenwich, then you can bet your bottom dollar that we all booked the same film and dutifully walked the 45 minutes to and from the cinema like a parade of mother ducks pushing prams. (As an aside, baby cinema is a great way to fill the morning if you're struggling – the tickets are cheap and no one minds if your baby screams.)

Becoming a lady who lunched

Rob joked a lot during the baby months that I'd become a lady who lunched. And, in a way, I really had – that's pretty much all I was doing. It sounds like I was a Sloane ranger, spending the day getting coffee, walking Greenwich Park, doing yoga or a baby massage class and taking myself and the baby out for lunch with my new friends. It sounds so deceptively idyllic when I write it down like that doesn't it? I can really appreciate how it must have seemed to Rob when he came home late at night after a long day of filming and I tried to impress upon him how tired I was, and, when he asked what I had done, all I could say was that I had been to a baby sensory class and then drank coffee at my friend's house with the other mums. Beyond just how much hard work it is being responsible for a baby 24 hours a day, 7 days a week, regardless of how much lunching with the ladies one does, I don't think Rob really understood the importance of those female friendships for me.

Female friendships are so different to men's friendships. For good or ill, men's friendships just don't seem to be as intense. Women need each other in a way that men don't seem to. There are whole studies that have shown that women respond to stress differently to men. By gathering with other women, we release the hormone oxytocin – the 'happy' hormone. Instead of the 'fight-or-flight' response largely seen in men, women have a wider repertoire of responses including 'tend and befriend'. Physiologically and emotionally, women rely on, and benefit from, friendships in ways men don't, and reap actual measurable health benefits by doing so – a decreased risk of dementia and lower blood pressure, for example.[8] Our 'tend-and-befriend' stress response may even explain why women consistently outlive men. Before the 'not all men' brigade comes for me again, I'm not saying this is a universal experience – lots of men have very good and deep friendships, but I think it's fair to say that women have a different dynamic. There's an interdependency in women's friendships that means you've got an inbuilt support network, a hive mind to reason your decisions out with, people who will not only empathise but also probably understand or have their own experiences to share. People who you don't have to contextualise things for because they already just 'get it'.

That group of mums was so much more than the classic cliché of ladies who lunched or a coffee morning of gossip. Those constantly-interrupted-by-small-babies conversations over coffee were like free therapy. I had a group of people who didn't try to tell me how much more tired they were than me. A group of people who were navigating these new waters too, whom I could ask questions of and express feeling to without fear of judgement or sounding like I was going mad. It was physical help sometimes too; many hands make light work and all that jazz.

At the very least, in almost all cases, someone's husband was being less helpful than mine, which I know is bad, but always made me feel better. However irrationally cross I was at Rob for whatever infraction, real or imagined, there was normally at least one partner who'd been more of an arse that day. Rob probably doesn't know how many times he was saved from one of my hormonal meltdowns by the fact that I had had a coffee morning and come away thinking, 'at least he's not booking a boys' trip when the baby's only 3 weeks old' because 'the baby doesn't settle for me anyways'.

I can't describe how much the 'find your tribe' or 'mama bear' sweatshirts make me want to do a little vomit in the back of my mouth, *but* that being said, FIND YOUR TRIBE. Find your parent friends. Any parent friends. Literally anyone will do. They don't have to be your best friends crying round your casket decades down the line. Hell, they don't even have to be your friends in two years' time, but find a group of women with potatoes the same age as yours and cling on to them like they're a life raft off the side of the *Titanic* because you'll need them more than you know. I don't know how mad or sad I would have been without my WhatsApp group to message in the small hours of the morning. I think I saw these women more than I saw Rob in the first six months of being a mum. He was working so much and they were all off on maternity leave with nothing better to do than meet me for yet another trudge round the park.

You can refine this group as time goes on – what started as eight of us at those first coffees got slowly whittled down as we got to know each other better beyond the camaraderie that comes from being the same prisoners of newborn war. You cannot afford to be fussy in those initial stages, though, so just find some people and get out of the house. If you don't do an antenatal class, this is going to be harder, but just keep turning up at baby groups and classes and always, *always* stay for the coffee afterwards. That's where you'll find your people. Just don't be that person telling everyone else what they 'should' do. Or how well your little cherub is sleeping. No one wants to hear it.

Filling the Day as the Default

As the default parent, especially in the newborn and baby stages when you're probably not working as well, you have both loads of time and absolutely zero time. One day, I remember almost crying with frustration that I had been at home all day but achieved almost nothing. The flat was a state. We hadn't gone anywhere. We hadn't seen anyone. I hadn't had a shower. I had no real idea, when asked by Rob when he got in, what I had managed to do for the last 12 hours. It was maddening.

I was used to being up and about. I like being productive. I used to leave for my teaching job at 7am to get a head start on the day. Since being on maternity leave, for want of a better term, I wasn't used to doing so little but also feeling so exhausted. The total lack of enforced structure sent me a bit doolally. (That's the technical term by the way.) In fact, the structure of your day completely changes: there's no putting on your nice work clothes, no getting your lunch ready, no popping out for a coffee mid-morning, no chat with your colleagues in the staffroom, no validation from a day's work well done, and no pay cheque at the end of the month.

I was so desperate to add some kind of structure to the day and feel like I was doing something of value that I must have tried every single baby class within a 10-mile radius. You name it, we did it. No matter how ridiculous. Baby massage? Sign me up. Baby yoga? Yes please. Baby Explorers? When do we start? The more deranged the better, to be honest. (And this is another thing no one warns you about before you have a baby – the classes that you'll be persuaded into because it apparently helps their development or their sleep or something like that.) It was a way to add what felt like definable value to my day – I had achieved something if we had been out and completed a class. Some of them even gave you a little certificate at the end of term – maybe it's the perpetual teacher/student mentality in me, but the thought of a little achievement certificate really got me going. Is it even worth doing if someone doesn't tell you how well you've done and give you a printed bit of A4 paper at the end? Exactly.

Whether my 3-week-old baby needed to be dragged across Lewisham to be stripped to her nappy and massaged at 9.30am every Tuesday remains to be seen. Actually, it doesn't remain to be seen – she absolutely did not. Rob and I had an argument one morning when we were running late for baby massage because she was sleeping, and I was arguing that we should wake her up and go. Rob was quite sensibly asking me what kind of crack I was on that I wanted to voluntarily wake up a sleeping baby to go to baby massage when she had absolutely no awareness of baby massage, or indeed any conceptual awareness of stress that would mean this tiny 3-week-old fresh human needed a massage. I insisted on going and, on cue, she screamed all the way through it and I came back home feeling thoroughly defeated by life. Not that I showed that – I wasn't going to lose this argument even if I did have a little cry in the toilets of baby massage.

Baby classes and activities are brilliant; however, they add up, especially when so many of them want you to sign your life away and book onto a whole term. Babies are notoriously unreliable little cherubs. It's almost guaranteed that, once you've signed that unbreakable contract in the blood of your firstborn, they'll decide that what they loved one week is physical and mental torture the next, and you'll be stuck either dragging yourself and your potato along every week so you don't 'waste' the money or having to write off the whole thing, which is so frustrating when you've already paid for it.

I took my eldest to a lovely music class, which you signed up for, termly, and she loved it. As she got older, she engaged with all the instruments, really paid attention and seemed to get a lot out of it. The teacher said she must have musical bones and, like the delusional sleep-deprived maniac I was at that point, I could have cried with pride at the little Mozart I had clearly birthed. When my second was about 6 months old, I signed her up for the same class without doing the trial week because I knew the class, had loved it and our first had thrived there, so we'd love it again right? Wrong. Very, very wrong. Our second did not vibe with group fun. She was not here for the camaraderie of a class. She quite frankly didn't give a single shit about the instruments or the softly spoken teacher. She just screamed from start to finish. Threw the instruments. Wouldn't stay in the circle. When she had thrown all her instruments, she crawled around the circle throwing the other babies' instruments. Eventually, when she had thrown everything that wasn't nailed down, she crawled to the shut door and just screamed at it, furious that she couldn't get out.

I was mortified. I did my best to contain her, to get her interested in the activities, but she wasn't having any of it. Worse than that, the other parents were not at all sympathetic. Normally, when your kid is kicking off, the other parents in the room are just so happy it's not their child behaving like a demonic banshee that you get little empathetic 'We've all been there' smiles. Nothing. Not a sausage. In the end, I was so hot and sweaty from constantly running across the room to wrestle her back into our spot before she stoved another child's head in with a maraca that I picked her up under one arm, grabbed my bag with the other and left. I cried in the car on the way home and we never went back.

Looking back, maybe people weren't as unsympathetic as I thought they were; maybe they were just focusing on their own child and weren't concerned about what mine was doing. Maybe I was just exhausted and in the midst of the hideous hot flushes from the postpartum hormones that no one warns you about and I lost my head. Either way, that was the end of my dream to form a mini Von Trapp family band. One musically-boned child was going to have to suffice.

My favourite kinds of classes were the pay-as-you-go ones, the turn-up-and-give-an-overenthusiastic-woman-at-the-door-of-the-church-hall-a-fiver kind of ones. It didn't matter if everything had gone sideways that morning and you didn't make it, because no one was expecting you. And when my youngest inevitably opted herself out of the group fun and sat by the door screaming again, at least it was a slightly different group of people each week to be mortified in front of.

Playgroups at churches are really good for this, and they'll almost always have coffee and biscuits too. The best ones don't even make you sing a hymn or something at the end – perfection. The least religious church playgroup near me is so popular that there's a queue down the pavement at least 20 minutes before it opens and, if you're not in that queue by then, you've got no chance. You're left in the one in/one out line. Berghain's got nothing on this playgroup.

I liked to map out my week so I had something I was going to try to do with the baby each day – not necessarily things I was beholden to if it all went to pieces that day, but a general plan of my week. I had a spreadsheet of every drop-in class or bookable-on-the-day activity in the area so that I could organise myself even when I was exhausted. I even put down whether it had parking or whether I could pay by card. That spreadsheet saved my sanity on the days when I had nothing to give but I couldn't stay indoors because it felt like the walls were closing in on me. You know, those days when you have absolutely no brainpower or energy to plan something, but you physically cannot stay in the house any longer because you're all going to end up just staring at the walls crying until someone comes home and you end up exploding at them because they've had the audacity to be out in the real world with other grown-ups.

Staying sane as the default parent of a newborn/baby is all in the preparation. I felt much better when I was busier – busier with the baby, but also once I started squeezing in little pockets of time for me to see my non-mum friends or have a tiny bit of time to myself.

A Quick Guide to Carving Out Time for You

Our understanding of the importance of self-care has changed massively, even in the last decade, and I think most of us can appreciate how key it is to make time for yourself and prioritise your needs sometimes. Which is absolutely how I feel, but that's so much easier when you only have to decide that for yourself. However, if you're at home with babies, then your social life, self-care and career are essentially going to be a committee decision because of the need to arrange childcare. It's then hard not to feel like you have to have a good reason for wanting or needing to do something. Or that you're being judged. Those precious parcels of time that the non-default parent has by virtue of leaving the house to go to work or their inability to produce milk out of their nips are so inherently ingrained in our understanding of parenting that, for the most part, I'm not sure the non-default even notices how easily they can schedule in having their needs met. It's easy to go to the barbers after work or pop out to five-a-side if you've already assumed your weekend is devoid of plans.

As a new mum, self-care is a seemingly insurmountable mountain, but establishing that time, rest and space for you to do your own things outside of work is so important. It will all change and shift in the reality of having a baby as you adjust to the new way your lives work and the new needs of everyone in the house, but if the horse hasn't already bolted, then it's worth trying to nail some of these precedents down now. By no means am I suggesting that you need to be doing everything you did before you had a baby, because having a baby is massive and takes all of you, at least for a time. Don't give yourself more stress thinking you 'should' be seeing friends more or keeping up with hobbies, but just introducing the concept of proactively protecting time or yourself into your pre-/post-baby discussions with your partner can help you carve out the time that you need, once you feel ready. Having someone else feed the baby, for example, releases so much pressure, especially if you're finding breastfeeding challenging, and frees up precious windows of time for you to have a bit of space while someone else assumes responsibility.

The non-default parent needs time too, of course, but the reality is that, while they might not recognise it as such, they are already getting lots of pockets of time to themselves just by virtue of leaving the house to go to work. Eating lunch undisturbed. Getting a coffee and reading their messages on the train. Talking to other people about non-baby stuff. I'm sure it sounds desperately sad to non-parents to be classing these things as 'self-care' time, but, in the early days of having a baby, they absolutely are.

So, please do have those conversations about who is responsible for what before the baby gets here, but also keep having them – because the beauty of children is it all *keeps changing*. What you needed one month is going to be different the next. What worked to keep you a happy, sane, healthy parent when they were 8 weeks old is going to be different when they're 6 months. They're different. You're different. Nothing is static when you've got a baby – they're changing all the time, so the way you and your partner navigate what you all need has to adapt and flex too. However your timetable looks, whether there's a nine-to-five, Monday-to-Friday job in there or whether your work is more erratic like Rob's, sit down every week or so and map out what the week looks like for both of you: when are you in and when are you out? When is your partner going to be home and in charge of the baby? When are they having their time and when are you having yours? Default parenting thrives in the 'We'll play it by ear' and the 'We didn't have any plans so I thought it would be fine to …'. You shouldn't have to spell it out, of course you shouldn't, but sometimes the quickest way to getting what you need is to remove all the grey areas. Lay it all out, make a plan and, most importantly, keep re-evaluating that plan, and you'll be fine. I believe in you.

3

TODDLERS & TANTRUMS

(But Sadly No Tiaras)

It feels like it should be easier having toddlers than babies and, in a way, it kind of is, but don't get ahead of yourself – the game's changed and you need to get your head around the rules your little cherub is now playing by.

Babies are physically a lot of work – your body is recovering from pregnancy and childbirth, you're exhausted from the sleepless nights, you might be literally feeding them from your own body and you're adjusting to the seismic changes that having a new baby has had on your career, your social life and your identity. Those tiny, insignificant, minor impacts aside, babies are remarkably portable. They're effectively a work-intensive Tamagotchi in a pram. Yes, they demand your input at any given moment of the day and night, but you can pretty much take them anywhere and they're going to behave the same way as if you were anywhere else. We accidentally took our eldest to a nightclub in Copenhagen when she was six months old and she slept all the way through …

Toddlers are a different kettle of fish. At the risk of being one of those insufferable people who I despise, telling you how easy you've got it when it feels the hardest it has ever been, the baby stage really is the easiest it's going to be for a long time. I know, punch me. I spent so much of the time when our eldest was a baby almost wishing time away because it felt like it would be easier once she could crawl or feed herself. When she was getting really frustrated at not being able to walk, I kept thinking to myself how much happier she would be when she could. And then she started walking at 10 months, which is insane. And the world fell in on itself.

The world's collapse might be a *slight* exaggeration, but when babies transition into being full-fledged toddlers, it suddenly becomes a whole different ball game.

What's That Coming Over the Hill ...?

A whole world of new places opened up once I had a toddler: soft play, trampoline parks, the cinema – the possibilities were kind of endless. And then I realised that, as much as the world had opened up, it had also become a lot smaller. I could now only go to places where I could entertain her out of a high chair and also where she wasn't going to hurt herself; well, hurt herself more than I could help it anyways because toddlers could hurt themselves in a padded cell.

The parcels of time I could get away with sitting down in a café or talking to another grown-up were now limited to how long she would sit in a high chair with some melty puffs. It doesn't matter how many stickers and toys you have or how many snacks you bribe them with, when they want out of the high chair or portable baby prison (aka the pushchair) then you're done. You're off, crouched like Quasimodo, following your tiny precious, now walking, potato around a soft play designed for someone half your height and twice your fitness, trying to stop them from careering into someone carrying a tray of scalding liquids or preventing them from climbing up a book shelf to see if they can fly. Toddlers are physically capable enough to get themselves around, but, developmentally, they've got about three brain cells rattling around up there. They know what they want and can physically just about manage it, but they've got absolutely zero understanding of what is going to hurt them or why perhaps they might not be able to do whatever insane thing they want to do. Immediately! Right now! NOW!

Toddlers can look so much like competent human beings that they trick you into a false sense of security. They may look like mini people, but they have none of the reasonableness of grown-ups. They can do so much more than babies can, but with no sense of their own impending doom. Toddlers also have no concept of societal norms – you can explain until you're blue in the face that they're not allowed to scream in a library or throw their pasta at other unsuspecting customers in restaurants, but there's no point because, and I can't express this enough: They. Do. Not. Care. So, it's important to remember you are not dealing with a rational human being. You're dealing with a teeny tiny terrorist, drunk on decades of unopposed power. The best-laid plans can be derailed in an instant by a toddler determined to have a bad day. And it is amazing how resolute they can be to seemingly hate everything and everyone around them, even though their whole world at that point has been shaped to their needs and wants. There's a list of approximately a thousand places I would rather be at 9am than a freezing cold trampoline park playing Disney songs on repeat (OK fine, the Disney songs I love). But here we are – because it's what she loved last week. And yet, there she is in the corner screaming at the wall for an infraction so small I cannot even speculate on what has drawn her ire.

Is it a bird? Is it a plane? No, it's Supernanny!

That maddening saying 'Fail to prepare, prepare to fail' is annoyingly apt when it comes to toddlers. A whole day can go to absolute shit in the blink of an eye if you don't have food to hand and they switch from blissfully happy to starving in a split second. There's no emotional regulation with toddlers, and trying to talk through their 'big feelings' is, in my experience, pretty pointless. If they want to be cross, let them. If you think there is something obviously wrong that's unsettling them then fine, try to solve it. If they're cold or uncomfortable, or, as is probably the case, deeply hangry, then you can try to sort that tangible problem to see if their mood changes, but, beyond that, I'm a big believer in just leaving them to it.

I tried to do the lovely gentle parenting thing I've seen on so many beige-toned mummy blogger's Instagrams and, when it works, you feel invincible. I'm so unashamedly desperate for any kind of approval that if I could see that my oh so reasonable and patient talking though of feelings was working with either of my girls, my voice would get unintentionally louder so people around me could see what a nice, patient mum I was being. That worked, I would say, maybe 1 per cent of the time when they were toddlers.

I know phone manufacturers are adamant that your phone isn't operating as a tiny M15 agent in your pocket, but I am convinced that mine listens to me, trying to talk to my screaming toddlers through gritted teeth, as my algorithm on Instagram and TikTok became almost entirely all clips of the myth, the legend, the Supernanny herself, Jo Frost.

If you're in the trenches of hysterical toddlers, I cannot recommend getting on the Supernanny side of TikTok enough. It's got everything: kids who are almost always behaving worse than yours (I know it's bad, but as long as there's someone else having a worse time than me, I don't feel quite such a failure), parents who are almost always handling it worse than you would have (again, I'm going to hell, and maybe I'm a hideous sadist, but misery loves company and it's nice to know you're not the only one feeling like they're incapable of making a good decision) and, lastly, in the holy trinity of good things from being on this side of TikTok, Jo Frost has an almost idiot-proof approach to toddlers: you just say it's unacceptable, no reasons and no explanations, then you put them in time out.

Toddlers are visceral, feeling-led beings at 1, 2 and even 3 years old. So, do something they'll understand: 'Your behaviour is unacceptable and, when you do that, you are removed from the fun. Or the fun is removed from you.' They might not understand much at this age, but they grasp cause and effect really quickly if you're consistent. 'Bite your sister and you can't play no matter how much you cry.' *Et voila*. This is so much easier said than done – I've spent 45 minutes trying to get my 3-year-old to stay on the bottom of the stairs for a time out. By the time we eventually managed three minutes, I couldn't even remember what she'd done and had to say sorry for. But we did it. And I think it helped. At the very least, it gave me a process to follow, which is half the battle when you're exhausted by toddlers and babies pulling you in a hundred different directions. Sometimes, you just need a simple plan to follow. It's the consistency that works, so, whatever feels right for you, do that and stick with it. Keep it simple and easy to follow, and at least when everything is chaotic and overwhelming you've only got a couple of steps to remember, not 92.

Embrace the 'Zen', even if it's fake

As well as time out, you also need to get really good at your 'I'm so unbothered I'm almost asleep' face for when your toddler is kicking off. Kids will have tantrums anywhere, and they don't care that you've spent a week's wages and your sanity trying to take them to Chessington World of Adventures, if they want to behave like a diva then they will. So, the sooner you get immune to or at least very good at pretending to be immune to your child being a maniac in public, the more freedom you'll have. That is by no means me saying let them behave how they want or avoid doing discipline in public (time outs/threats to take away their iPad; not smacking obviously), it's saying that your world opens up a whole lot more as a default parent if you're not afraid of going to places and it going wrong.

If they kick off, get yourself a mantra – whatever works for you – repeat it and just wait it out. I've got a friend who repeats, 'I love my life' over and over. Rob's favourite is 'This too shall pass.' I had a brief spell with Buddhism when I was younger because someone I really fancied was a Buddhist and I did what any sensible person does and promptly took it up too. In my defence, he was very handsome. I don't really practise any religion at all now, but there are bits of Buddhism that have stayed with me and one of those is a meditation chant that was particularly catchy. Turns out that it was buried deep in my psyche because that's what comes out when the kids are being feral and I'm trying to look totally neutral and unbothered: 'Nam Myoho Renge Kyo.' No idea what it means now, but it has a nice flow to it. Choose whatever works for you – just something you can focus on while the chaos reigns around you.

I used to stare into the middle distance repeating my mantra in my head as my child screamed. So, next time it's all going wrong, the kids are kicking off and you just want to sit down in the middle of the supermarket and cry, find something in the distance to focus on and start your mantra. Sure, you might get home and cry then instead, but you'll have left the house at least. Left the house *and* not given in to tantrums? That's top-level default parenting in my book. You might feel really self-conscious; I definitely did and still do. However, I would rather people were staring at me holding my nerve while my child has a tantrum than watching me give in. Judge my feral child all you like, but I'm not going to give you any reason to judge me if I can help it. It's very liberating getting to the point where, outwardly, you are keeping your cool in the face of all provocation. Fake it till you make it baby. That's the official advice here: keep on keeping on.

Keeping the Juggle Alive

I'm not going to go on and on about how hard having a toddler is (I probably am), but it's important to remember that, by the point they're a toddler, you've been parenting for years. Literal years. Your reserves are depleted in a way that you couldn't even fathom pre-children. Sure, you're in a routine and you're probably used to a lot of the ways in which your life has changed. The clothes you used to wear before pregnancy that you were going to get back into have sat for so long at the bottom of your wardrobe that they've been slowly phased out each time you've done a charity shop bag. The colleagues who you were so close to they were almost your best friends, you now haven't spoken to properly in months because last time you saw them you felt so out of the loop with what was going on at work and it felt like you had nothing to contribute that it was almost less painful to take a real step away and focus on the more immediate here and now. You can't really remember the last time you went on a proper night out because not only do you have to find babysitting for your precious little babies, but you're probably so tired that all you really want to do is stay in and sleep. Or, as I found out the very hard way, if you do go out, you're so overexcited that you drink way too much and forget that the babysitter isn't there in the morning and you're absolutely going to have to parent your small children, just feeling a hundred times worse than you normally do. Your life has changed so seismically and for so long that it is getting harder and harder to remember who and what you were in the time before your children.

Despite all the gloom I've just spouted, I actually really loved when the girls were toddlers. Once our youngest was out of the little baby stage, I had a 3- and a 1-year-old who were both walking, kind of talking and I could take for days out. However hard it was out of the house, I preferred being out and about with them rather than being in all day. I'm fully cognisant of the level of rose-tint the glasses I'm wearing currently are, but I have so many glorious memories of the silly days out we'd go on that I'm feeling all nostalgically maudlin as I write this.

Recruit some help, any help

It's easy to find a bunch of first-time mums to knock around with when it's your first. You do antenatal classes or you go to the baby groups and loiter near the mums who look the least insane until they invite you to join them for coffee. By the time you're on baby number two, it's harder to find people who are doing the same thing you are as everyone's at different stages. I had a 2-year-old and a newborn. Our 2-year-old wasn't in nursery yet, and so she still needed entertaining in the day, but I also had a newborn in tow. She wasn't really the issue as, for the first few months at least, I could just bring her wherever we were going to entertain the eldest, but I needed friends who understood that my needs with two were different than with just a newborn or just a 2-year-old, that I couldn't always do the things we did with just one.

I had a brilliant friend who only had a 2-year-old, but was so blessedly kind that she would always take charge of both hers and mine if I needed to sort the baby out. I don't think I would have been out of the house half as much without her and I'm grateful whenever I think of those times. There are apps now like Peanut or Hoop (caveat: I haven't used these personally) that help you find activities or hook up with other mums who might have the same combination of kids as you do, which sound great, but they weren't out when my two were weeny.

I was also really lucky that my mum lives nearby and had recently retired when I had my eldest, so I had company and help for a lot of the time when the girls were younger if I wanted it. My elder sister also had her first baby when my youngest was 1, so I want to really caveat this before it sounds like I've morphed into one of those smug super mum types who just loves telling everyone all the marvellous things they were managing to wrestle their progeny to every week, with I HAD HELP AND COMPANY.

Taking babies and toddlers anywhere is always going to be chaos, so find someone who leans into that. I made one of these seemingly eternally unflappable friends at one of the less ridiculous baby classes I took my eldest to. She was exactly what I needed – someone who gave me permission to let the chaos happen and embrace it as far as possible. I didn't worry what the house looked like when she came round, because she got it. And she didn't judge. Not even secretly. She made me so much braver as a mum and I'm so grateful to her, and for her friendship. By no means did these days out always go to plan, but it didn't really matter because no one was expecting them to; we just kind of cracked on with it and tried to laugh it off as best we could.

Admittedly, that was slightly harder when, one morning in deepest darkest January, we'd all gone for a Gruffalo nature walk in the woods near us. What's a Gruffalo nature walk you ask? Well, in our infinite wisdom, we printed Gruffalo pictures off and took it in turns to run ahead and hide them on the path for the kids to find while we recited as much of the rhyme as our sleep-deprived brains could remember. That's what I mean about finding yourself a slightly mad friend – I don't think I would have done that by myself, but we had strength in numbers.

Sounds lovely and wholesome doesn't it? Out in nature while the 2-year-olds ran around gleefully finding clues? Apart from the fact that the fresh-out-the-womb newborn I had strapped to my chest started screaming at the exact point the 2-year-old I'd foolishly decided to potty train in deepest mid-winter said she needed a wee. In the woods. Wearing a full puddle suit and wellies. Now, I had one of those little travel potties with me that look like an animal, which I tried to get her onto in time, but, to absolutely no one's surprise, I didn't manage to get her puddle suit down before she started weeing. The baby was being dangled in the carrier, fully upside down and perilously close to falling out as I bent over the 2-year-old. Then, to really round off a successful five minutes for me, her welly got stuck in the mud, she fell over and her sock got wet. We all ended up back at the car covered in varying degrees of mud and, if I'm honest, wee, but it almost seemed funny because I had my mate with me.

You need people around you to pull you out of the trenches. Yes, there'll be days when you get home and, quite frankly, question your sanity and why the fuck you took two 3-year-olds across London in rush hour on two tubes to see Andy and the Odd Socks, and paid extra for meet and greet only for your child to scream hysterically in every photo as you desperately tried to reason with her out the side of your clenched jaw, *but*, in hindsight, those days were so much fun. Ridiculous and stressful. But fun.

I know having help made it infinitely more possible to attempt (key word there: attempt) going on days out, which I'm not sure I would have been brave enough to try on my own. Whether that was my gloriously positive to the point of being delusional friend or my mum and sister, when it's all going to shit, if you've got other adults there, there are just more hands to get on deck to wrestle the kids into submission. Or, failing that, at least there are other grown-ups to mutter, 'for fuck's sake' to under your breath or to stop you crying on the train when a middle-aged businessman, who really should have known better, asked me to get my mid-tantrum 1-year-old to 'keep it down'. If you're someone who has EVER huffed and puffed disapprovingly at the parent of a toddler mid-meltdown, then please know I detest you, and I wish your sandwiches be eternally soggy. Just be kind.

Grand Days Out Versus a Hard Day's Work

The memory of that man telling me off on the train has brought back the reality of a lot of those toddler days out. The problem with toddler days out, much like the baby ones, is that, if you're not actually there, then on paper they sound glorious. Especially when being relayed to a partner who's been at work all day and is probably looking for a way to feel hard done by. It's difficult to make it sound like hard work when what you've done is got the train to London and had a nice lunch in Leon with your mum and sister, then had a mooch around Tate Modern. Or even just been to the park on a sunny day and sat on the grass eating a Mr Whippy.

Those innocuous little sentences hide a multitude of sins, however. I can't tell you how many times I've cried out of deep-seated frustration after either getting in the car or coming home that, despite all the effort and planning, and sometimes the ludicrous expense, it felt like a total failure of a day. Sometimes, everything just feels like it's all going so very wrong: the children are inexplicably furious at everyone and everything, no one's eaten the lovingly prepared packed lunch you made, they also didn't like any of the three overpriced options you've bought from the café, you left the house in a state and it's still a pit when you get back in, you've been out in public all day dressed like a bag lady because you were on the bottom of the priority list this morning and every single coffee you tried to have today was lukewarm at best. And has been for three years. It's just one facet of being the default parent – the expectation that you need to be all things to everybody all the time, and sometimes, despite the best-laid plans, it's just impossible to please everyone.

It's then very, very hard not to despise your partner when they get home and make a throwaway comment about the state of the house, or the lack of dinner, or even something as innocuous as 'Oh, that sounds like a fun day out' when you tell them what you did. The problem with being the default here is that you *have* to fill the day. You have to get from A to B doing something. There's no getting around the fact that you've been in charge of small children and, even on the most halcyon of days when it has all gone perfectly right, it's still mentally and physically exhausting. It's just hard to convey that it's work still, when your partner's been at their literal work.

Rob would be really jealous of some of the days I spent with the girls while, conversely, I would, at times, be so indescribably jealous of him getting to go off for a day at work or, in some cases, whole weeks away. It's really hard to muster sympathy when he's tired from work sometimes when he's been at New York Fashion Week or on safari in South Africa. Last year, he was away overnight 112 times for work, which I get is time he's missing the girls, but it's also time when he can just be an independent adult. The grass can definitely feel greener sometimes as the default and, as much as I wouldn't swap those early days, it would be disingenuous to not reflect the reality of a lot of that time – that it was really, really hard. If you're with your toddler all the time then it can feel like sometimes you're pouring from an empty cup and you're not getting that time at work to be an independent adult and fill yourself up so you have something to give tomorrow when you've got to do it all again. It really takes a toll on your mental and physical reserves.

Rob just couldn't understand sometimes why I was so triggered by no one listening to me the first, third, ninth, twenty-eighth time I said something or being totally sensorily overwhelmed some days with the chaos in the house. What he wasn't seeing was that, however much work might have been hard or tiring, he had still had many hours not parenting to recharge as an independent adult, to rebuild his resilience to the ravages that toddlers can wreak upon you. Asking kids to do something 11 times is almost funny when it's only a few times a weekend. When it's every day, though, it's wearing. You start to feel like you're going mad; can anyone even see me? I've had full-on existential crises about the meaning of my own existence getting the kids ready for pre-school, and that is impossible to recreate with a non-default, however involved they are. I mean, Rob's never made up a whole 'no one listens to me' song, sung in an increasingly frenzied and borderline offensive faux Italian accent as a means to vent some frustration. I would argue that, even if your partner was a present and active participant every evening and weekend of the year, there's no real way to recreate the impact that being in charge of children seven days a week has. Even if you leave them for a long weekend and bugger off on a girls' holiday, which I highly recommend by the way, they'll still find a way for it to have been harder for them for three days than it is for you *all* the days. Give yourself credit for just how hard it is to both fill the day and also not lose your marbles as the default parent of a toddler.

The Ultimate Mantra

When it's all going to shit around me and my usual Buddhist mantra isn't working, snippets of this poem – 'If–' by Rudyard Kipling – often pop into my head from the repressed depths of A-level English Literature. I know it's about the horrors of warfare inflicted on soldiers in battle. However, if you reread it through the lens of motherhood, it speaks to me more than it ever did in the classroom…

Read: toddlers losing the plot.

If you can keep your head when all about you
Are losing theirs and blaming it on you,
If you can trust yourself when all men doubt you,
But make allowance for their doubting too;
If you can wait and not be tired by waiting,
Or being lied about, don't deal in lies,
Or being hated, don't give way to hating,
And yet don't look too good, nor talk too wise:

Don't let people looking or tutting get to you – you're an island of serenity.

Don't engage with irrational toddlers – it's not worth it. Sometimes silence speaks loudest.

Let go of what you wanted your day to be. Be flexible, roll with the punches and take your wins where you can.

If you can dream – and not make dreams your master;
If you can think – and not make thoughts your aim;
If you can meet with Triumph and Disaster
And treat those two impostors just the same;
If you can bear to hear the truth you've spoken
Twisted by knaves to make a trap for fools,
Or watch the things you gave your life to, broken,
And stoop and build' em up with worn-out tools:

Parenting will always be both – don't put too much stock in either.

You can't win an argument with a toddler; it's not worth trying.

Your old life is gone, but you're building yourself a new one.

Just keep on keeping on – don't get bogged down in what's happened. Just keep swimming.

If you can make one heap of all your winnings
And risk it on one turn of pitch-and-toss,
And lose, and start again at your beginnings
And never breathe a word about your loss;
If you can force your heart and nerve and sinew
To serve your turn long after they are gone,
And so hold on when there is nothing in you
Except the Will which says to them: 'Hold on!'

Toddlers are a battle of endurance and resilience. You've got to outlast them.

keep your cool no matter what's going on around you. Don't let people and what they're doing or not doing affect your decisions – keep your train on its own track.

If you can talk with crowds and keep your virtue,
Or walk with Kings – not lose the common touch,
If neither foes nor loving friends can hurt you,
If all men count with you, but none too much;
If you can fill the unforgiving minute
With sixty seconds' worth of distance run,
Yours in the Earth and everything that's in it,
And – which is more – you'll be a ***Mum****, my son!*

If you can do this, you can do ANYTHING.

STARTING SCHOOL

(And the Horror of Being Back in the Playground)

Right, so you've survived being pregnant, made it through the newborn phase and ridden out the tantrums of the toddler years – you've finally arrived at the point where they go to school. For five days a week, for a lot of the weeks of the year, you're now going to get six and a half hours of government-mandated child-free time, GUILT-FREE, because they have to go. This isn't a choice you've had to agonise over; this is a fait accompli. This is almost every civilised society in the world literally saying, 'this is best for your child'.

Before the homeschool brigade come for me, absolutely mainstream school does not suit every child. Just like one-size-fits-all clothes are a myth designed to make all non-waif people feel gargantuan, so is a one-school-system-suits-all. If it doesn't work for you, and you're happy to educate your child yourself, then more (absolutely insane) power to you. To each their own. But after the Covid-19 lockdown and attempting to teach just one of my children at home, with the help of her school, her actual teacher on Zoom and my retired teaching assistant mum bubbling with us to help, it is definitely not my own. (And I say that as a fully qualified former teacher who used to impart knowledge to whole classes of teenagers semi-successfully. It's an entirely different ball game when it's your own child.) My own is sending them to school the second the doors open on the first day of term and letting the highly trained professionals who have a bit of emotional distance from the darlings in their care take over.

Your child starting school comes with a whole new load for the default parent to manage. You've spent the last four and a half years with your identity being intrinsically tied to theirs and suddenly you find yourself with six and a half hours a day without them, but wait, don't get too comfortable with whatever series of the *Real Housewives* you were about to shamelessly binge, school admin and playground politics wait just around the corner for you ...!

In hindsight, when the kids started school was when the default parenting load really noticeably diversified. Up until that point, so much of the default parenting burden was very physical: who stays at home, who goes back to work, feeding, changing, days out and all the other thousand things you do as the default parent that, by this point, you've pretty much got your head around. But then the ground shifts beneath you and what's expected of you as a parent, especially a default parent, changes again. When the girls started school, it wasn't just the explosion of extra physical tasks that had to be kept on top of, like homework and uniforms, it was the mental and emotional load as well. Starting school catapulted me into a new phase of default parenting identity, where I wasn't just the girls' mum, I was a school mum now. There's a whole raft of new challenges to face: friendships, schoolwork, bullying, parent friends, school admin and so on, which all fall disproportionately on the default to manage. This shift really challenged me as a default parent, and I've questioned my decisions and second-guessed my judgement so many times since they started school. You shouldn't underestimate the impact that all these additional tasks and things to think about and make decisions on have on you. It can be maddeningly frustrating and really lonely sometimes doing most of the logistics of parenting by yourself as so much of it is repetitive grunt work so you never really notice the progress you're making.

As I was writing this chapter, I realised that the girls starting school sent me on much more of an emotional deep dive than perhaps I realised at the time. I was obviously prepared for a lot of emotions – my babies were growing up and, without sounding like a familial despot, the almost total control I had over them was slipping away. Before the girls started school, I knew all their friends, because their friends were the children of my friends. I made sure they didn't spend loads of time with lunatic children who punched one another because I simply did not arrange play dates with said lunatics. What they experienced in a day was up to me because I was the one in charge. I could make sure as much as I could that I was on top of them being kind, empathetic and open-minded little humans.

For almost five years, I was responsible for what they ate, wore, read, watched and did every day. Those days add up to hundreds of thousands of decisions that all feed into the creation of the tiny human you're making. So, when school steps in and takes a lot of those decisions out of your hands for those six and a half hours a day, five days a week, that control starts slipping out of your hands and it's terrifying. Suddenly, they're coming home with names you've never heard before, telling you things you haven't taught them. That's not an entirely bad thing, of course. I know I can't teach them everything they need to know by a long stretch, but it's still a massive adjustment, especially as the default parent.

There's less 'advice' in this chapter for default parents, and perhaps more about the seismic shift your role and identity goes through (again!) when your children start and move through school. So, take from it what you will – maybe there's some helpful advice in here for you; maybe there'll just be a flash of recognition that it's not just you who felt like that or struggled in this way; or maybe all it'll do is reassure you there are parents out there (me) coping infinitely less well than you and you can take comfort in not being the most unstable one at least.

Adding to the Default Decision Load

I really thought that parenting would get easier as the girls got older, because they would be physically so much more capable and I would be correspondingly less responsible for keeping them alive. If anything, though, the responsibility keeps feeling weightier, because the decisions feel more impactful. Apart from family and the home environment, there's nothing that has a greater influence on your children and the people they're developing into than school, and the pressure to make sure it was a positive experience for them weighed heavily on me. It started with touring the schools in our area and filling out the application forms. I have to admit I lost my head a bit choosing schools. I know enough from teaching in an 'Outstanding' school, albeit a secondary rather than primary, that the Ofsted grade isn't the be-all and end-all that Ofsted would have you believe. The teachers I worked with were amazing and went above and beyond after school and at weekends to get the kids' grades way beyond their predictions, but it came at a cost. I'm not convinced, though, in hindsight, that it was always in the kids' best interests to be put through a one-size-fits-all system to get them five A to C grades that the school could use on their league tables.

Rob was formally assessed and diagnosed with dyslexia in 2024 after struggling his whole life in formal academic settings, and I've witnessed first-hand how that experience of struggling still impacts him. I was absolutely determined that I wanted the girls to go somewhere that would look at them as a whole person and prioritise their well-being instead of just focus on the relentless pursuit of educational progress. Of course, I want them to do the best they can, but not at any cost. I'm happy for them to go at their own pace and in their own way. If that means that little Brenda, or whoever the resident class boffin is, is a few reading stages ahead at the end of Reception, then so be it – it all levels out eventually.

School infinitely adds to the default parent's administrative load. When we knew which school our eldest was going to, I automatically assumed responsibility for making sure she had her uniform and all the other thousand and one ridiculous things she needed. I was the main point of contact for the school and it was my number that went on the class WhatsApp. A lot of this was just practical – I was at home and Rob worked a lot, so it made sense that I was the first port of call for both arranging school stuff and for the school to contact. As a default parent, you're just so much more involved in the day-to-day admin and decision-making that school demands. It's much easier as the non-default to go with the flow when so many of the decisions and interactions required in the school year are already a fait accompli. The default parent physically does so much more of the actual interacting between school and home that they have to be on top of things, or at least pretend to be.

Working out what's going on when and what your precious little dumpling needs is like being on an episode of *The Crystal Maze* where you move from one baffling room to the next being asked to complete tasks that are increasingly incomprehensible and physically impossible. My brain's never worked harder than at 6.20am on any given weekday when a vague memory flits across my consciousness that someone needs something today. Who that someone is or what they need, however, is another matter. Suddenly, you're searching through three different systems trying to find the key bit of information, which will unlock the crystal. I mean, why would you put everything in one place? That's no fun! Put some of it online. Email some of it. Put some in a bottle and send it out to sea. Put their homework on nine different apps, all with different logins, which were sent out weeks ago on a scrap of paper that was lost before it even left the school grounds. (If you work in a school and especially if you are in charge of the admin, I'm asking really nicely, I BEG of you, in fact, please, please put all the information in one place that's searchable by date or key word. We're too tired and addled to keep up.)

My advice here? Split duties with the non-default parent as much as you can and make the information idiot-proof and accessible. Accessibility is half the battle here – I'm not saying you have to go full TikTok organiser mum with colour-coded wall planners and laminated organisers, but find somewhere you can put the timetables/info on the wall so you can point wordlessly to it instead of answering a thousand stupid questions. Email the office and make sure they have your partner's contact details too to make sure they're getting every godforsaken email and school post as well. Even if they're not actioning it, they should have to at least read it.

Cosplaying Your Own Life

Nothing in the entire time that I've been parenting, and default parenting especially, has made me feel more like I'm cosplaying as a mum than the girls starting school. Up until that point, you could parent pretty much whichever way felt best for you, with what felt like limited outside judgement. You were friends with the people you wanted to be friends with, not because of proximity but by choice. What I realised when they started school was that I'm not sure I'm ever going to feel old enough or competent enough to be in charge of my children. When your children start school, you not only have to interact with the professionals who work in the school and present yourself as a competent grown-up adult who absolutely can do addition using the bar model method (if you don't know what this is then SAME GIRL), but you're also going to have to speak to the other parents. Suddenly, you're back at school yourself, making friends as a grown-up in situations where you have little control over who you're making friends with. When you start a new job and befriend the colleagues you work with, you're at least starting off with a shared interest in whatever career you've chosen. When you find yourself standing on a school playground, not as a child, but as a fully-grown adult, you've got nothing in common with any of these people other than you happen to all live in the local area and this was probably the school that was the closest to your home – and you have to suddenly make more small talk than you've ever made in your life thus far. I just wasn't mentally prepared for how many people there would be and how much talking I'd have to do. There is just so much more small talk than I was anticipating and small talk is so deeply not my forte.

I've spent most of the last decade or so unlearning a lot of the unhealthy dynamics I had with my own school friends, and whether it's a hangover from never quite feeling like I was doing the right thing or not, I'm just not very confident making friends as a grown-up. I'm not antisocial; I've made really good friends everywhere I've worked and I have the best group of friends a lady could ever want now. But there's no getting around the fact that I am absolutely terrible when I first meet people. I'm horrendously socially awkward and simply cannot quiet the running ticker tape of negativity in my brain telling me, *What you said was stupid. You've offended everyone now. What you're saying isn't even making sense. No one cares. What are you even talking about?* … and so on ad nauseam.

I'm 39 and very firmly a grown-up person. I own a house. I've had jobs where I've been responsible for important things. I have a manual driving licence. (I'm ostensibly more of a grown-up than Rob by that metric as he only has an automatic licence and, believe me, I never let him forget it.) But, as a parent, I don't understand how old I've got to be or how long I've got to do it for before it feels like I'm not pretending to be a 'good mum', playing giant overgrown dress-up.

I've sat in countless open evenings by now or across from the girls' teachers at parents' evening and I'm looking around at the other parents sitting there thinking, 'Does anyone else feel like they've got no idea what they're doing or is it just me?' Because everyone always looks and sounds like they've got their shit together. When the teachers ask at the end of the appointment, 'Do you have any questions for me?', all I can think is that, of course, I should have questions, I should have something to ask shouldn't I? But it's a blank. Or when a teacher goes, 'As a teacher, you'll probably know this, Mrs Beckett ...' and I'm thinking, 'Do I? I don't think I do!'

The girls have been at school for five years now and there's only been one time I've felt confidence in myself as a parent at a school thing, and that's because I wasn't acting as a parent really. I went into full teacher mode on a school trip I was helping with. We'd gone to central London on the train and I was in charge of a group of four children. My actual tone of voice changed for the duration of that day. Suddenly, I wasn't my eldest's mummy, I was Mrs Beckett again and the power 100 per cent went to my head. The teacher, who was actually in charge of the trip, and not me, as I had to remind myself, complimented me on how well I was managing my group. There's very little point to this story other than I just had to tell you, as so rare is it nowadays that I feel confidence in what I have done.

What I've learnt as a parent, which has been really driven home by the years since the girls have been at school, is that there will always be people who look like they have their shit together – the trick is to ignore them. There will always be that parent who knows the answer already, whose child is always in the right uniform, with the right homework. It's taken me a long time to get here, and I'm still not all the way there, but, honestly, it's an absolutely joyless endeavour trying to keep up. Like the ladies who managed to turn up to baby groups in a cohesive outfit with make-up on and their hair done, there are parents in the playground at pickup who look and sound like real-life people again. Sadly, that's still not something I've mastered, but that's life. That's parenting. I'll get there eventually. Or maybe I won't. Maybe I'm destined to look like that pigeon lady forever, with nothing interesting to say.

Whatever level of 'school mum' you're capable of being, all you can do is your best. There will be fellow mums and default parents in that playground who are your people and who can relate and who will support you through this period – you just need to persevere through the thousand awkward kids' parties until you find them. And, once you do, cling on.

Getting Involved ... (Don't)

Rob and I are the antithesis of one another when it comes to what we each deem superfluous to requirements. For the much more socially comfortable of the two of us, Rob would quite happily forgo all social engagements and school events. Whereas, even though I am so uncomfortable and out of my depth with it, I'm the driving force behind being involved in school because I understand it's necessary. Yes, sometimes it feels like a necessary evil, but it's necessary nonetheless. I don't want my children to be social pariahs who never do play dates or birthday parties, and nor do I want the school to think I'm a disinterested parent.

Anyway, it's impossible to keep entirely to yourself at your child's school, and you wouldn't really want to as you're going to be spending many, many years with these people and their children in the future. Believe me, if nothing else, you're going to need that parents' WhatsApp group at 6.30am when you can't remember if it's a PE kit day or not.

That being said, the day I join the PTA is the day you can shoot me. That's a step too far. Volunteer at your peril – they don't want your input, they want your labour. You've got enough to do default parenting, don't add to your load. Obvious caveat before I get banned from the PTA Pimm's stall at sports day next year: I appreciate all the work they put in to hold events for the children and raise money for the school. I couldn't and absolutely wouldn't do it, so thank you to them, and more power to you if you enjoy it. You big power-hungry weirdo.

I've learnt over many years to accept that, try as I like, I'm simply not capable of being the class rep parent who manages to somehow corral the 101,783,242,769,230,293 emails from school into a coherent plan for the week. I was co-class rep for the Reception year when my eldest started, but I was very much there for moral support only. I was in charge of the vibes. Of which there were none. The only thing I can say I was truly responsible for across that whole year was suggesting vouchers for the end-of-term teacher presents because there are physically only so many 'Thank you for helping me grow' plant pots one individual person can have in a lifetime, and that number is zero. Speaking as a teacher, vouchers is absolutely a hill I will die on: GIVE TEACHERS VOUCHERS.

Playground Politics

As the default parent, you're going to be the one on the front line dealing with friendship issues, playground politics, play dates from hell and talking to the school about issues while trying not to come across as the neurotic parent who all the teachers try to avoid. Ask any teacher, primary or secondary, and they'll immediately have to hand the names of the parents who are forever emailing in with inane questions and increasingly ludicrous complaints. There won't be a second's hesitation. I haven't taught in almost a decade and I can still remember the stupidest emails I had from parents. I've had to talk to the girls' school a few times about things over the last few years and I'm so deeply paranoid about becoming 'the' parent at the top of 'the' list that I always end up writing embarrassingly gushing cards at the end of the year thanking them for not thinking I was neurotic.

At primary school especially, the probability is that the issue you're most likely to come up against is the travails of friendships.

Unfortunately, they seem to be a rite of passage for all children at some point, and there is not much you can do to avoid them completely. You've had so much influence over their friendships up until they've started school and, suddenly, you're being regaled at 3.35pm with dramatic tales of some shit that's gone down that day or who's been particularly naughty. There was a little spate of graffiti in the girls' school where someone was writing the 'f word' on the wall in the infant school toilets and the drama with which this was relayed to me by the girls was nothing short of Oscar-worthy. I have my suspicions about who was responsible, naturally, but I shall take that to the grave – and to the smaller breakout WhatsApp group of school mums who I trust, obviously.

Toilet graffiti aside, something I've grappled with is what to do when I think, or I know, a friendship isn't a positive one. What do you do if your child comes home and they've made friends with a kid you're quite reasonably convinced is a sociopath? I'm not talking your average garden variety of weed kid – there are little weeds in every class (and, if we're honest with ourselves as parents, as much as we'd like to live in a state of blissful denial, at some point it will absolutely be our child being the little weed – it's going to happen and that's OK). I'm talking about when it's a repeated pattern of behaviour and a kid is consistently just not very nice. That's when my parent 'spidey senses' go up. If your child's coming out of school repeatedly saying that the same child is upsetting them, then you feel like you've got to do something. The problem is, what? What can you do that's not going to escalate the situation or, worse, lead to an actual parent-on-parent confrontation in the playground? I've been in situations at pickup when you could physically feel the tension crackling across the playground and, when I'm not one of the participants, I bloody love it. The passive-aggressive messages on the class WhatsApps? Glorious. Shoot me, I love the drama.

As the default parent, I'm the first person the girls see when they come out of school most days and, if they've had an issue with someone in school, I'm the one who hears about it first. It's much easier to be a calm and rational non-default when the story's being relayed to you second-hand by the default that evening, than first hand in the playground by an 8-year-old who's trying not to cry because the same kid who was a weed last week about her football boots has now called her new glasses ugly.

Dealing with problems at school

I've split the parents at school into two groups in my head and the distinction is small but weighty: the 'absolutely not my child' and the 'maybe my child' camps. Doing a mini audit of the mums I'm friends with, I think we're all in the 'maybe my child' camp and, in my judgement, that's where you want to gravitate towards. It makes sorting out problems a thousand times easier if you're dealing with people who are even slightly open to the idea that, perhaps, just perhaps, their child might have behaved in a way that wasn't 100 per cent practically perfect in every way.

To the point I possibly throw my own children under the bus and blame them too easily for things, I am firmly in the seeing something's kicking off and immediately asking if one of mine is responsible camp. It's much better to be out ahead of the game – you'll look proactive and realistic as a parent, which is all you can do really.

I get it, I've also been tempted to disavow responsibility for my children when they've done something appalling out and about, but people aren't stupid – they know which child belongs to who and everyone else is judging you for not getting involved, much more than they were for the original behaviour. I've spoken to parents about things that have happened at school who are either totally oblivious to what's going on or in such a state of wilful denial about their child's behaviour I've actually wondered whether there's some kind of diagnosable psychological problem happening. Either way, they say it takes all sorts and you'll definitely meet all sorts when your children start school.

If you're having issues at school with either a parent or a child, and if it's a repeated pattern of behaviour, I am a massive fan of a little FYI email to the teacher. I know from working in a school myself that it is so hard for schools to do anything without a body of evidence to back them up. When a teacher talks to a parent, even the most determined 'not my child' parent will struggle to refute a collection of emails from different people saying largely the same thing over a period of time. You don't have to kick off massively and demand changes be made *right now*, just flag incidents as and when they come up and let the school build a pattern of behaviour. Put the onus on the school, who can manage the situation far less emotively than you can. Teachers are there because they care for the well-being of your child and they don't mind questions or concerns being raised, if done in the right way. Knowledge is power and, as brilliant as teachers are, they can't do much if they don't know what's going on.

Grotty friends are a bit like early preparation for when they get grotty boyfriends or girlfriends when they're older – you can tell them they're not good for them until you're blue in the face, but, ultimately, they've got to learn those lessons themselves. Better they learn them now, so, by the time they get those knobhead boy/girlfriends, they can set healthy boundaries.

The importance of finding people who just 'get it'

There are going to be amazing days at school when your kids have achieved something they've worked really hard at or had a really fun day with their best mates. These are also going to be countered by days both you and they find really hard. When they're struggling with their homework and you can't get them to engage with it, or they've fallen out with their friends and don't want to go into school, or someone's been really horrid to them and they're upset, you, as their parents, and the default parent especially, are going to need a bit of bolstering yourself. For you to prop them up, you're going to need propping up yourself sometimes too.

Rob is brilliant and supportive in a myriad of ways that I really value, but, to be honest, this is where I've really appreciated beyond words the group of school mum friends I've made. My eldest started school in Covid, so the classes were bubbled and the parents didn't socialise at all really because Boris said no (it'd be nice if he'd listened to his own rules, hey, but we move). So, while I'm friendly with everyone and they're all really nice, I didn't make proper mum friends until my youngest started, and that group of ladies has saved my sanity on more occasions than I can count.

If you are a fellow default parent and you're losing your head a bit, my mum friends and I refer to it as going on a 'spiral'. Mum friends can relate to the spirals more effectively than our non-default partners can, perhaps, because they're also on the front line of the school dynamics, and they know who we're talking about when we say '*that* child'. Without having to explain who everyone is and who the parents are, and the history of incidents, you can actually get through a conversation without all the footnotes that are required when talking to your partner.

Another benefit of having a group of mum friends to vent to is that you're much more likely to be venting to them while your child's in school and not within earshot. Because while children can't hear their own name being shouted from 3 metres away at a volume more appropriate for a ship's foghorn, they mysteriously develop the hearing abilities of a bat when you start talking about children or parents they know, and you best believe, at some point, normally at the most organ-shrivellingly awkward moment, they will repeat what you've said.

My 6-year-old asked me what an 'S person' was because a child at school had told her, 'My mum says you're an S person.'

Ten points if you can see where this is going … I told her to ask the child as I didn't know, and then thought no more of it until she very cheerfully announced the next day that it meant she was a 'little shit'. Now, I'll take responsibility for a lot of words the girls know. I've taught them some colourful vocabulary by accident that, in hindsight, perhaps would have been best to keep as an inside-my-head thought. However, 'little shit' isn't *my* insult of choice. As it turns out, though, it is the insult of choice for one of the other school mums in the year.

So, as a warning, if you're going to slag off another child from school and, believe me, I do sympathise with that urge, make sure you're not doing it in earshot of your kid. Because I will absolutely send an 'FYI email' about you calling my child a little shit and, at some point, you will have to sit in front of both the parent of the 'little shit' in question and the 'I'm not angry, I'm just disappointed' class teacher and explain exactly what you were thinking. I have so much second-hand embarrassment from that conversation – and it wasn't even me in trouble – that it's thoroughly cured me of any temptation to let rip about other kids while the girls are within 100 metres of me. Key piece of parenting advice here: pick your audience wisely. Loose lips sink ships. You can't trust your kids to have your back and you can't trust some school parents not to be shamelessly slagging off your child in front of their own.

I highly recommend finding some mum friends with children in older years as well, as they'll have a perspective you don't have and can rationalise some of the processes from a longer-term view than you can. Mum friends will also be empathetic to you slagging off your partner when they've not helped with the school run or packed the wrong uniform.

You might be with a partner who splits the mental load of being on top of school stuff, as well as the physical necessities of getting the kids up and out to school on time, but the majority of default parents are doing it largely by themselves, unless they've specifically asked and probably got everything ready in advance. Sometimes, when the children have taken three hours to go to bed because 'they've forgotten how to go to sleep' (a real complaint from my youngest), they've refused to get dressed for school because their trousers are 'too soft' (again, a real complaint from the youngest), they've apparently forgotten how to respond to their names and, despite getting everyone up and ready horrifyingly early, you're still struggling to get everyone out the door and into the car as the clock creeps menacingly towards the absolute latest you can leave without having to go in through the school office walk of shame, you need to go and have a coffee with other people who just 'get it'.

Get it without you having to explain or justify anything. People who get just how utterly demoralising it can be to feel like you're battling to be heard by your own family. Grounding yourself periodically with other people who can make you feel validated without you having to explain or justify things over and over is really important as the default parent.

Ask the Teacher

If, like me, you've ever really wanted to ask teachers what they *actually* think about things, but don't want them to judge you at parents' evening, then this section is for you. Despite being a teacher myself, I was genuinely curious to know the answers to these questions – I know my own answers, but was I the anomaly?

These questions were submitted by fellow defaults and I asked a cross-section of teachers across primary and secondary schools to answer them anonymously.

Do with the below what you will. Whether these answers influence what presents you get for your little darling's teachers, or reassure you that your cherub is definitely not the worst behaved out there, or perhaps you'll now leave parents' evening actually understanding what the teacher was trying to tell you, enjoy this insight into the thoughts of teachers.

I've always wanted to know what they actually think about all the gifts they get. Especially the home-made ones. If someone's baked something for them, do they eat it?

I'd never eat a baked good given to me by a child; sorry, but bleurgh. I've seen them cook at school. My immune system is good but not that good!
Mrs S, primary, Devon

Things the children have made, like a card or picture, are actually cute and there is always a spot on my desk for those bits, but if it is edible it's going straight in the bin!
Mrs F, primary and secondary, Kent

I LOVE the presents!!!! I get a haul every year around exam time and it is like Christmas.

I've had students bring me home-made Eid or Diwali treats and they are also really proud when you compliment something from their culture. I feel honoured to be included. I'd feel terrible to refuse when somebody has spent time making something with you in mind.
Miss B, secondary, the Midlands

Do they gossip about parents? About kids?

Yes, we talk about the children and families, but I wouldn't necessarily call it 'gossiping'. Understanding the family helps you understand a child and support them appropriately.

But sometimes you do just need to get things off your chest to a colleague or some light-hearted relief after a tricky day.

'Ooooh, I wouldn't have put them together.'

'A's mum completely blanked me this morning after that awkward phone call about their behaviour.'
Mrs S, primary, Devon

OMG, parents provide great gossip!!! Parents think that teachers need to know about parent disputes with other parents, parent playground arguments and definitely when one parent is in a relationship with another kid's parent, so the parents tell the teachers this info all the time!
Mrs F, primary and secondary, Kent

We are absolutely not meant to, but we of course do. We need to vent because people are frustrating!!!

However, I do not gossip about the serious stuff – if a student has a mental health issue or if there is domestic violence in the home or something like that.
Miss B, secondary, the Midlands

Is there a list of parents where as soon as you see their names on an email you just KNOW it's going to be bullshit?

Most definitely! Most parents just want to be listened to and know that you have the best interests of their child at heart, which we ALWAYS do, but some parents do make it hard to like them. I've been screamed and yelled at and threatened by parents, which is not acceptable in every other professional setting so why do they think it's acceptable in a school?
Mrs S, primary, Devon

There are always those parents that make me groan when I see another email pop up from them! The ones who moan, the ones who tell you their life story and the ones who are 'just checking' information that went home in the letter yesterday! Always the same parents!
BUT the worst kind are:

Parents who think the teacher's role is nothing but sorting out their child. I think they forget we have a class of 30 kids. I had a mum call the office and ask for an 'emergency conversation'. I left the TA with all 30 children and went to take this emergency parental call, with all sorts of 'emergency' scenarios running through my head. The emergency turned out to be that the mum was in M&S and wondered if I could check the size of jumper her son was wearing and call her back so she can purchase the right size!!!!
Mrs F, primary and secondary, Kent

I don't keep an official list, but I know which ones … and if I see the name I'm like, 'OK here we go again.' There are a lot of 'little princesses' who couldn't possibly do anything wrong. And the parents call to fight their corner and you're on the phone for hours.
Miss B, secondary, the Midlands

What's the naughtiest thing a kid's ever done?

It's a close call between set a treehouse on fire and cut the wires to the electric gate of the staff car park so no staff could leave at the end of the day.
Mrs S, primary, Devon

Maybe not naughtiest, but definitely the funniest:

When I was teaching at secondary, there was a lovely garden in the middle of the school ground, the area where all classrooms looked out on, and marking all the flower beds were white stones. Two kids decided to rearrange all the stones onto the grass in the shape of an ejaculating penis so, by lesson changeover, those kids on the higher level got a wonderful bird's eye view!
Mrs F, primary and secondary, Kent

I had a Year 10 brought to me by the deputy head because she was falling around all over the place (clearly drunk). We searched her bag, found nothing, but she couldn't stand up or walk in a straight line.

Next day, one of her friends told us she'd been drinking neat vodka from a water bottle while in PE; she'd then thrown javelins while drunk!!!!
Miss B, secondary, the Midlands

Finding human poo in discreet places within the classroom/ resource containers is always fun.
Mrs H, primary, Northumberland

Is homework actually useful or just a pain in the arse to set/mark?

A: It totally depends what it is. I would never set homework just for the sake of it. In primary, times tables and phonics are always worth practising at home and, in my opinion, reading with your child should happen every day.
Mrs S, primary, Devon

Annoying – takes ages to set, then you have to mark it or chase up kids who haven't done it!
Mrs F, primary and secondary, Kent

Our school has an 'only set homework if it furthers progress' rule. So I rarely set it. I think most teachers will agree it's bullshit … it doesn't further progress, lots of parents do it for their children and it's just extra workload to mark.

School is a lot, it's a long day of focusing in a classroom. Children need to be able to switch off and have a break in the evening. And parents don't need the extra stress of forcing them to do homework.
Miss B, secondary, the Midlands

How do you deal with pushy/difficult parents?

You play along for a while and slowly gather evidence to give them. It has to be done tactfully though, or you can be accused of 'picking' on their child. But sometimes they just can't see it and never will. You as the teacher will always be wrong.
Mrs S, primary, Devon

Biggest bit of advice I would give is don't assume you know everything about your child – they behave differently in different situations.

All children have the capability of being nasty to each other, especially when behind a keyboard. And they do not have the brain capacity for self-control like most adults do. And as they grow and their bodies get full of hormones, it affects their mood and how they interact. So just because you've raised them a certain way, doesn't mean they won't be horrible to each other.
Miss B, secondary, the Midlands

It's actually one of the most frustrating parts of the job because when parents won't work with you, it's an impossible and vicious cycle. I've had some children at 4 years old say, 'Don't care because my mam/dad says you're a liar', and where am I meant to go after that?
Mrs H, primary, Northumberland

How do you approach parents' evening with kids who are massive shits? Is there a code language?

Sometimes, we'll ask for a member of the senior team to be in their meeting – that probably means we're worried about meeting you. I tend to just give parents the facts and ask them if they have any questions or worries. If it's getting off topic, I'll tactfully wrap it up and get up and open the door. If it's really nasty, I used to just end a meeting and say we'll make a further appointment to meet with the head teacher. These meetings can really affect the mental health of a teacher, so please be kind.
Mrs S, primary, Devon

'Assertive' = bossy.
'Leadership qualities' = takes over at any opportunity.
'Bubbly' = uncontrollable and bouncing off the walls.
'Sense of humour' = class clown.
Mrs F, primary and secondary, Kent

'X needs to learn how to resist distractions in class' = your child will not shut up and listen.

'X needs to follow instructions properly to ensure they're working safely' = your child doesn't listen properly in practicals and has nearly set my lab on fire.

'X needs to hone their revision technique' = your child is not doing well in assessments because they haven't revised.

'X has struggled to navigate their friendships' = they've caused drama by being horrible to others.

Miss B, secondary, the Midlands

There is absolutely a code language and key phrases we consistently use to communicate:

'Highly enthusiastic in voicing their ideas during carpet time' = can't stop shouting out.

'Enjoys engaging in their chosen activities' = only interested in doing what they want to do and when they want to do it.

We're also well-trained in the shit sandwich, sandwiching something bad in between two good things so we don't make parents cross.

Mrs H, primary, Northumberland

5

MORE THAN JUST A MUM

Being a mum is the greatest privilege of my life, but that doesn't mean that it's not really hard. Your identity takes a real hit as so much of what made you, well, you, has been changed seemingly irrevocably. The totality of the change to the very physical reality of your life is huge – everything now revolves around the kids and it's hard to see beyond that. It can seem like your old life is so far behind you, and a new reality where you're your own person again can seem impossibly far off, especially when they're small. The biggest challenge for me since becoming a mum has been managing the competing factions of my identity, balancing how much I love being a mum with the desire to be 'more' than just their mum. How do you reconcile the parts of yourself that feel like they're at odds? When you want to be 'more' than 'just a mum' again, how do you transcend that label and manage the inevitable avalanche of mum guilt at wanting 'more' when you already have so much?

The Illusion of 'Free' Time

Leaving aside all the suppressed childhood trauma, which you've been forced to revisit when your child starts school, you're also left to deal with the added 'free time' you're suddenly getting. You've got time and space to think for what feels like possibly the first time in literal years. Which, on paper, sounds great. But I spiralled. And I spiralled HARD. Speaking only for myself because everyone's situations are different, I didn't know what I was meant to be doing now the girls were at school and ostensibly needed me 'less'. I had time! Guilt-free time! I should be doing all the house projects I needed more than 48 seconds in a row to complete. I should go back to work! I should go back to university! I should volunteer somewhere! Suddenly, all the frustrations I'd been harbouring about Never. Having. Any. Time all came to the fore simultaneously. That's no mean feat for your brain to process.

You've spent the best part of four or five years working full time as a default parent, let alone any other work you've been doing as well. You've been on call for your kids (and partner) for years by this point and, suddenly, there's a chunk of the day when someone else is legitimately in charge of them. If you're anything like me, what happened immediately then was the little voice I'd been largely placating with 'I'm too busy keeping these humans alive' suddenly had enough headspace to really ramp up the volume.

If you've read this far then I think from the earlier chapters it's fairly obvious that I struggled with the loss of my professional identity and the all-encompassing nature of being 'a mum' when I had the girls. Just as I was reconciled to that new role and leaning into it, suddenly the goalposts shifted and the parameters of my life and role changed again when they started school and left what felt like a void that needed filling. I'd spent years telling Rob I was feeling like I was losing my identity and now I had an opportunity to get that back and, to be honest, I was at a total loss as to what to do next.

School isn't glorified childcare – there's a lot of pre- and post-work involved: uniforms, trips, homework, reading, drop-offs, pickups, holiday activities ... Which means you need to work out what it is you want to do now you have 'free time', and also manage the extra admin involved in making sure that everyone still has what they need when they need it. In an ideal world, this load would be shared equally between the parents, but we all know that this rarely happens. The default precedents are set and they're especially resistant to evolution if you've been in that dynamic for a number of years before you go back to some kind of work.

I'm incredibly fortunate that I had the financial freedom of choice here. I'm not ignorant of that fact, and I'm certainly not complaining. Just perhaps recognising that the apparent wealth of choices on offer sometimes makes it feel like it's difficult to make the right one.

It all felt overwhelming, and some of those choices were a fool's dream, as the logistics just wouldn't have worked. I am painfully aware as I type this that there are people making full-time jobs and small children work for them. People using every before- and after-school club going, utilising a complicated web of friends and family to make pickups and drop-offs work, who, somehow, some way, managed to pull childcare arrangements out of seemingly thin air and go back to work. And to those people I take my metaphorical hat off. Because that requires Pentagon levels of coordination and physical and mental gymnastics to get everyone covered and you still manage to work a full-time job? HERO.

Whichever way you slice it, though, it's pretty impossible to not feel like you're simply being stretched too thin to be effective – not being a good-enough mum but also not a good-enough employee; pulled in too many different directions to be effective.

When I left work, I rationalised it by telling myself that I would be the BEST mum I could be. I'd teach them to read before they started school. I'd cook all their meals from scratch. They'd do loads of enriching activities. The house would be impeccable. I fell down the rabbit hole of comparison and saw other mums achieving what looked like the impossible, and it gave me a yardstick by which to measure myself, of all the things I 'should' be achieving if I wasn't working. Of that list, I think I maybe achieved, oh that's right, none of it. Not only were the girls 90 per cent pasta, tinned sweetcorn and frozen fish fingers, they also definitely could not read before they started school. I tried. I really did. I ordered flash cards and phonics packs, and we did them for a bit, but I soon discovered that they did not want to listen to their mum because, even at 4 years old, they could tell I didn't have the foggiest what I was doing.

If your children are happy and healthy, then you've done your job well. I just wish I could go back and tell myself what a good job I was doing then – not that I would have believed future me.

Wanting more and the default parent guilt

Aside from the overwhelming love you have for your children, the overriding emotion of default parenthood, which we've touched on, seems to be guilt. I've spent the last 10 years of my life feeling bad about something. I think it's become such a permanent fixture in my brain that I almost don't recognise it anymore. There's an undercurrent of guilt that's permanent, whether that's the guilt at not working full time anymore and using the qualifications and experience that I worked so hard for. Or the guilt at feeling resentful of Rob still getting to go and have his career. Or the guilt at feeling bored or unfulfilled by the Groundhog Day-esque treadmill of daily life as the default. Or the guilt of having mini-people who you love more than absolutely anything in the world and still feeling like it's not enough for you. Or the guilt of being off work when others have gone back and feeling lazy that they're somehow managing to achieve everything you have that day, but also furthered their career and earned a pay cheque. Or the guilt that you're somehow letting the sisterhood down by being a stay-at-home mum when we've fought long and hard for the right and provisions to be able to go back to work. Or the guilt when I did try to do something for 'me' and then I couldn't do something the girls wanted me to do.

I felt that more than Rob. Though there were very good financial and health reasons for me being the default parent, it meant that, if there was anything I wanted to do outside of that remit, I had to rearrange our lives to accommodate it. Which, while I know Rob would have been supportive, felt like a load of added pressure to make sure the disruption was justified. Justified not just from a financial perspective, as whatever I was bringing in would have to be more than whatever it would cost to cover the childcare we would need, but also on a practical and emotional level. Without blowing my own trumpet too loudly, the pillars of our family life are built upon me as the base. Those pillars would be hella wobbly without me as the default making sure everyone's foundations are taken care of. Everyone always has what they need because I make sure of it. Everyone can leave the house in the morning and go off to school and work because I've created those conditions. If I removed myself from the equation, or even just added in my own pillar to the structure, it'd make the foundation so much less stable for Rob and the girls. So it has to feel justified, and that pervasive default guilt is really hard to appease.

I felt guilty for staying at home and doing 'nothing', but then felt guilty for wanting more when I had so much. From a feminist perspective, I also wanted the girls to see me as more than just a mum. I want them to live their lives without limits and I want to be a role model for that. But I also don't want them to think that being a stay-at-home mum is a bad thing if that's what they choose. Because I have chosen this. And contrary to appearances in the midst of what seems like thousands upon thousands of words of whingeing, I am happy with this choice! But I also want to be more. I want to use my brain more than I do some days. I want to have something tangible I can hold up and say, 'This is what I do and this is what I've achieved.' I want them to be able to tell people what their mum does, not just their dad.

Maybe it's because I hadn't been working before the girls started school, but I felt like I didn't have anything to contribute to conversations that wasn't about the girls or Rob for a long time, and yet I was meeting all these new people, almost all of whom were still somehow managing to be in the midst of these important and interesting careers while still parenting. Theoretically, the school playground should have been the place I could most comfortably be 'just a mum' and stand proud in that. Instead, I felt myself slipping back into that old spiral of feeling like I had nothing of my own to contribute.

It's very much a me issue, rather than an anyone else issue. Apart from two individuals who I've met through Rob's work things, who shall remain nameless, not a single person has ever made me feel less than (and you'd better believe those nameless people are so firmly on my shit list that there's nothing they could do to redeem themselves). Those instances stand out because they're the exception rather than the rule. It's so hard to remember that in the middle of a playground talking to what feels like hundreds of new people, though, without the comforting fail-safe 'What do you do for work?' conversation to build from, as saying I was a teacher almost a decade ago doesn't quite cut it.

Being my very own personal Marie Antoinette, I want to have my cake and eat it – that's the wrong phrase, I know, but roll with it; I'm enjoying the image of me in a gigantic wig stamping my foot about wanting to be Mrs Super Stay-At-Home Mum while also a boss bitch somewhere in a mystery company I'm yet to set up.

Anecdotally, I've spoken to so many of my fellow defaults and it's a sentiment that's mirrored time and time again – across the working board. Defaults who have gone back full time. Defaults who've gone back part time. I've got friends who've set up their own businesses, very successfully, and, even there, in people who I'm looking at admiringly, the frustration seems to be mirrored. The frustration at wanting, needing even, to do something other than be 'just' a mum, but then feeling guilty for that feeling. The frustration at knowing you have so much more in you that you could be giving somewhere, but not knowing where to direct that, or not being able to fully commit to it because you're the default. Your focus, your abilities, your energy are being constantly divided in a way that just isn't a consideration for the non-default parent. Imagine for a moment what you could do in a working day if you weren't trying to also do everything in your physical and mental default load.

Whatever it is we're doing as the default, it's hard not to feel guilty for something. So while it's probably not the most therapeutically correct approach, if you're going to feel like a bad mum anyway then you might as well just do what you want regardless. Ignore that guilt until the voice is quiet enough to be put back in Pandora's box and you can crack on. It's much harder work to be a good parent than a bad one, so if it feels like hard work then it probably means you're doing a good job. I've come to a realisation that, for me to be a good parent, I'm going to feel bad about almost anything I do that isn't 'parenting', but, conversely, I'm a much better and nicer mum when I've had some time and headspace to myself.

Going Back, or Not as It Happened

The longer I stayed off work, the harder it seemed to be to make the decision to get back into it. And when I did, it wasn't quite the triumphant return I'd envisaged. Perhaps because teaching is one of the 'vocation' careers that we're so often told is understaffed and badly paid, I just assumed, arrogantly so in hindsight, that I would be able to walk into a job when I wanted one. Given our family dynamic, I was willing to wait for a job I really wanted to come up, one that would work with Rob's schedule, maybe a couple of days a week part time so that I could still do the majority of the childcare/pickups, but I'd have my foot back in the door at least. I also wanted a school that was a different culture to the others I'd trained or taught in. I loved those schools and I adored (most of) the boys I taught; however, they were not easy schools and I was keen to maybe work somewhere where it was less behaviour management and more teaching.

Just such a unicorn job came up when the girls were in Years 1 and 3, in a lovely private girls' school nearby. Two days a week teaching girls. In a school where the head teacher said, 'behaviour management isn't really a thing here; they just behave because they know they should'. Perfect. Sign me up. Except they did not sign me up. The day of the interview was categorically one of the worst days of my life. And that's from someone whose body has regularly tried to shit itself to death in public places. So, when I say it was bad, I'm not exaggerating. I'd been out of teaching for eight years at this point and it showed.

Teaching interviews are a strange beast – they go on for flipping ages. You normally teach a lesson while two teachers from the school observe at the back, writing little notes about you. Then, you have a tour of the school with a pupil who asks you innocuous little questions for an hour, but who will absolutely be asked for their feedback on whether you're a lunatic or not and, to top it off, there's also a sit-down interview with the head of department and/or head teacher. In this instance, they did both, so I was there for four hours of constant scrutiny, give or take, and at no point can you relax unless you say you need a wee and go and hide in the toilets for as long as you can get away with. I was so nervous I had what I can only assume was a malfunction in the matrix and couldn't remember how to even start my own PowerPoint, and one of the teenagers had to show me which button to press. I told off a girl twice for talking, who, it turns out, relies primarily on lip-reading, but no one had told me, so I was delivering instructions behind her head and she was having to get her mate to repeat them to her. To top it all off, the head of department had to stop me mid-answer in the interview to tell me to take a deep breath and calm myself down. And I couldn't remember one single sensible question to ask at the end of the interview.

It was what I can only describe as an unmitigated disaster. Hours upon hours went by and I could see it spiralling out of control, but couldn't get myself together to regroup and actually show them what I can do. Because I know I'm a good teacher. I just need more than four highly pressured hours to show it.

To say that knocked my confidence is probably an understatement. I'd thought so nostalgically about the halcyon days when I was teaching that to be shown a glimpse of something I really wanted and then for it to not happen was quite depleting. I talk to the girls a lot about resilience and trying again if at first you don't succeed, and I really struggled to take my own advice, but I think a lot of defaults can empathise here.

It's hard going back to anything you haven't done for a while, let alone years. Even though it's largely in our own heads, it's really hard not to feel like you've lost your touch. Whatever it is you did before children and becoming the default, the longer you're out of it the harder it is to feel competent going back into it. So, what's the answer? Who knows, to be honest? I haven't attempted another teaching interview. I perhaps threw the baby out with the bath water and decided that this was a sign from the universe to be brave and take a stab at a business idea I've had for a while. I'm not reinventing the wheel; I just want to make big bags for mums.

I enrolled in a short course at the London College of Fashion, which was a lovely two weeks commuting up to Westfield where, suddenly, I felt like a whole human again. I met people as an adult who didn't know me. Didn't know Rob. Hadn't known me as a teacher. Didn't know me as a mum. Zero expectations. And it was marvellous. Until it came to the end and I was suddenly going to actually try to make these bags. And that's when that insidious little voice piped up again ... *What a self-indulgent thing to do. Spend all this money on a vanity project. Why do you think you're special? Why is it not enough for you to just get a normal job? Why not just be happy with what you've got? Why not get a teaching job, which you are actually already qualified for?* I think the longer I was a default parent and a stay-at-home mum, the larger the spectre of having to 'succeed' at whatever I went back to loomed. If I was going to not be at home, if I was going to make everyone's lives more difficult, then it had to be worth it. It had to be impressive. It had to be worthwhile.

Define 'worth' though. What are we achieving by constantly placing expectations on ourselves to have 'succeeded' or for things to be 'worthy'? It's exhausting to constantly put yourself through the rigmarole of trying to be all things to all people, all the time. That's taken me a long time, and ultimately a couple of unexpected hospital stays, to learn. Admittedly, being blue lighted to hospital because you've stretched yourself too thin is a fairly dramatic reaction, but it was definitely effective. If you don't have a helpful stress-flared autoimmune disease to be the canary in the coal mine, let me help. You. Cannot. Be. All. Things. To. All. People. And nor are you expected to be.

If you've found yourself, through choice or circumstance, as the default parent, you are already achieving an absolute innumerable number of things on a daily basis. If you're managing to do that while going back to work in any capacity then you're smashing the proverbial out of life and default parenting. Just because a lot of your labour is invisible, that doesn't mean it's not there. I see it. And all the other defaults see it. It might not feel like it in an empirical tangible sense, but you are achieving. It might be unseen. It might be unfair. It might feel like your brain is slowly turning to mush, but you're in there and we see you.

Don't feel guilty for prioritising your own needs, and try as far as possible to remove the financial weighting. It's hard to justify to yourself or anyone else why what you're doing is valuable if it's not bringing in as much as your partner, or if it's not bringing in anything at all, but if it's important to you then it is important.

I felt for a long time that I didn't have my own personality anymore. Everything I did felt centred around Rob and the girls. Their hobbies became my hobbies. Their interests were my interests. Their needs were greater than my own. My role as a nurturer and facilitator trumped everything else I needed or wanted to do for many years, but that role has evolved and, while those aspects are still there, they've definitely changed. The girls' needs are less all-encompassing, there are whole chunks of time now when they don't need me in the very immediate physical way that they did and it's allowed my brain a bit of space to think again. To think about who I was before, and who I am now. And, most importantly, who I want to be. That can feel daunting as hell after so long just ploughing on, making sure everyone else has a full cup.

If I have any advice here it's to start slow. I think I had so much pent-up – energy isn't the right word as I was shattered – but pent-up something or other that, as soon as I got a little window of opportunity, I probably threw myself a bit too hard into anything and everything. I was applying for jobs I knew I wouldn't take because they were full time and I couldn't make the childcare work with Rob's job. I have at least four half-finished applications floating in the ether of the internet for different master's degrees that I didn't submit because, logically, how was I going to be in Brighton studying the role of the communist party in the American civil rights movement while also taking the girls to school? I had a chaotic scattergun approach, simultaneously trying to work out how to do all the things I wanted to do as well as the things I thought I should be doing, on top of still doing all the work I was carrying out as the default.

Don't be like me: take a breath and take a beat. Because it didn't help the nasty little voice at all. By trying to do everything at once, all I did was give it more ammo. More things I hadn't achieved! More things I'd 'failed' at! Just be kind and realistic with yourself. These are self-imposed expectations and no one really cares if you're not meeting them other than yourself. Just try to sit with this, and actually take on board that it is OK to want more. It doesn't make you a bad mum, it doesn't make you ungrateful.

Give yourself the grace you'd give anyone else

Unless you're one of my two mortal enemies or the mum who called my kid a little shit, then I'm always a hundred times nicer to anyone else than I am to myself. If I were speaking to any one of my default parent friends, I'd say that anything that brought them satisfaction, sparked joy or made them feel like a whole person again was worthwhile.

As defaults, we place a huge and unachievable expectation on ourselves, far higher than we place on other people. This constant battle of guilt versus need is exhausting. The energy and headspace we give the guilt at feeling very valid, common feelings is an actual act of insanity when you lay it out. The hours I've spent with my friends haranguing ourselves for our wrong decisions, for our perceived failures, for not doing 'more' with our already impossibly full lives is so pointless.

Now, I'm very aware that this is very much a 'do as I say not as I do' situation, but stop looking at what everyone else is doing or achieving because the grass is always greener. You might be looking at someone who went straight back to work and is three promotions deep in their career now and feeling envious, but there's a good chance they're looking at you wishing they'd had more time to be at home, or vice versa.

So, much like an air stewardess (Virgin Atlantic, of course – they're the best ones with the snazziest uniform), this is me giving you permission, if you need it, to put on your own oxygen mask first. You cannot be a good parent if you have nothing to give. Whatever makes you happy, whatever makes you feel fulfilled, whatever fills your cup, try to carve out some time and headspace to do it. Because you'll be a better mum for it. Perhaps by the time this book comes out I'll actually have some of those big mum bags, but currently I have a self-printed certificate from the course I did and a couple of very bad samples to show for my troubles, and maybe that's enough for now.

The Working Default

It's all well and good me complaining about being the default, because, given Rob's work, there's little else I could be really. What happens, however, when the demands on your time are much more even? When you're both working? I rounded up a couple of my fellow defaults who have gone back to work in a formal capacity to get their take on it.

If you're both working, does that division of labour tally up with your available time? Does one of you inevitably end up default parenting, despite both working?

I'd make a conservative estimate that we split the parenting workload 70/30, possibly 80/20. However, I would say that J thinks that difference is less.

The reason for that is he doesn't know a lot of what I do. The visible stuff, the physical drop-offs and pickups, for example, he gets, but so much of what I do isn't physical or seen, and that's what swings the 70/80 per cent over to me. Even with what he's doing, it's generally because I've asked or organised for him to be doing it. And then I can't actually tick it off as done, as I've had to ask, remind, chase and check that it's been done and done properly.

J's much more black and white with his work. Work is work, and he's working. I'm also working, however, but I'm also stretching my capabilities and time to accommodate both parenting and work when needed. What J would say is that I make work for myself, and that's because I think sometimes mums do emotional labour that isn't maybe strictly necessary. For example, our son was starting swimming at school for the first time so I was getting his kit together and I realised that his goggles were maybe a bit babyish for Year 4. He hadn't said anything, and they were technically fine, but I was aware he was with his peers and I wanted him to feel confident, so I replaced his goggles with more grown-up ones. That wouldn't have flagged with J at all. Even though he'd obviously have no issue getting him new goggles, he would just wait until it came up, whereas I'd rather pre-empt the issue entirely.

I don't know how to even it up really – it's not that J wouldn't do more, because he would, but there would be a real pushing through the pain barrier process where I'd have to accept I was still having to do a lot of the admin around tasks, a lot would slip through the net and it would feel very chaotic. I'm not sure that it would feel worth it, especially if it started impacting the kids.

Mrs S, an educational consultant who works five days a week, four children

We initially decided on who would work more days because my leave was better financially, so it made sense for me to be off more. I also wanted one of us to be around for the first year developmentally, and, while we would have split it more evenly in an ideal world, it was more practical financially this way. We agreed that both being back full time while they weren't in school wasn't feasible for our jobs or what we wanted for the children. My work was more flexible and family-orientated, and going part time wouldn't impact my promotion prospects like it would have my partner's.

As time's gone on, we've both agreed we'd like more of an even balance, though – I'd like to work more and he'd like to be around at home more, especially when the children are still young and need us so much more. I'm looking to increase my hours when an opportunity comes up to do so, and he's trialling working four days a week to get a better work–life balance.

We tend to split the workload not by who has the time, rather by skill and preference. So, I have oversight of the children's activities and friends, and delegate as needed – this is partly because it led on naturally from being off initially on maternity leave so my organisation of the children's admin just continued without much discussion, but I also like the social side. I also tend to take control of the laundry and cleaning as I'm at home more to be on top of it, and I also have my system that I like and it creates more work to delegate that to him. He'll cook whenever he's home and definitely takes the lead on the more practical elements of the house, like DIY or maintenance. It's quite a traditional split when I think about it, but out of choice.

I think we have a pretty even split of the physical workload, that roughly follows our working patterns. It's important to him that he's very involved and can have his input into decisions and so on, but it's hard to properly divide that up evenly when I have been, and still am, currently around more than he is. A lot of the time it's just easier in the short term to do it, than try to explain what needs doing and why. We'd split it more evenly in an ideal world, but that would need a much wider cultural shift that just isn't there at the moment – workplaces that prioritise output rather than full-time or in-office working for promotions and so on, as that makes it much harder for parents to split the time more evenly even if they want to.

Mrs P, a clinical psychologist who works three days a week, two children

So, anecdotally at least, there you have it. Defaults are defaulting everywhere, whether you're back at work or not. It's just maybe that extra shade more maddening.

6

REMEMBER YOU'RE ON THE SAME TEAM

Something I've heard a lot, and definitely experienced, is the 'roommate stage', and it rings so true for the post-baby years of my relationship with Rob. I couldn't love that man more and there is no one else on Grealish's green earth I would rather be with, but, at times since we've had the girls, I just do not have the bandwidth to be his partner in the same way I was before we had them.

Having children fundamentally changes the relationship that you had when it was just the two of you. When it's just the two of you, there's a spontaneity to your lives. You have so much time, space and energy to think of the other; to spend quality time, to talk, to experience things together. You also have lots of free time to spend with your friends, to explore your interests and to just be you. How do you reconcile your relationship with your new reality as parents now everything comes secondary to this beautiful little human you've made? It's an enormous undertaking to merge everything you needed as an individual and everything you had as a couple with this new dynamic. Obviously, your life and relationships are going to change – the whole family dynamic has shifted. It's no longer just the two of you; there are whole other humans in the mix – tiny little ones who you have to keep alive. I just didn't realise how completely and for how long.

I'm 10 years into being a mum and it still feels like swimming upstream sometimes trying to keep the romance alive. The demands of children are so total that, at points, it can feel like you're ships passing in the night and all your energy goes on just keeping all the balls in the air. One of you always has to be on duty, as it were, which makes it really hard to carve out time for each other and remember who you were before kids. Watching Rob become a dad has been one of the greatest privileges of my life. He's incredible at it, and so utterly selfless in his prioritising of the girls and our family over his own needs and wants. However, while I love him more than I ever have, in all the years we've been together the time I have to show him how much I love him was probably at its lowest ebb when the girls were smaller in all the years we've been together. And my daily available headspace is still taken up with the needs of the girls, the house and keeping our lives functioning. The needs change, but the demand does not.

Feeling 'Touched Out'

Having children is a uniquely physical experience. When babies are small, you are physically holding, comforting, feeding or changing them for so much of the day. You can have the most chilled baby in the world (not me, but I hear they exist), but we've all had those days when they just won't be put down, those days when it feels like you haven't had something not touching you for more than three seconds. It evolves as they get older, but the physicality remains. As toddlers, they're holding your hand, clambering into your lap or lying horizontally across your bed kicking you in the face while you try to sleep. My girls are 10 and 8 as I write this, so they're well out of the toddler years, but they still love a cuddle, lying on me as they watch telly, wanting to sit on my lap, stroking my hair or asking for arm tickles. And I love it. I could breathe in the tops of their heads all day, but all that physicality feels like it needs balancing somewhere. It's delicious and lovely and I wouldn't swap it for the world, but it's also overstimulating physically. I want to give the girls everything

I have, which means that, sometimes, there just isn't enough left for Rob.

Sounds harsh, but it's true, and he's a grown-up who's adult enough to understand the realities of the situation and know that it isn't personal or permanent. I can't say to an 8-year-old, 'Mummy doesn't want to cuddle you right now because if anything else touches my skin today I'm going to scream', but I can absolutely say to Rob, without worrying about planting seeds of childhood rejection and trauma, 'Get off me right now because I'm so touched out I feel like I want to gouge out my own eyeballs.'

This isn't me saying shout, 'GET OFF ME' to your partner whenever they come within 100 metres of your person, but you are absolutely allowed to feel touched out and overstimulated. Having children around you all day is a lot for your body to process. It's a constant mental and physical test of endurance and if, for a few years, there isn't enough for your partner when they get in then they're going to need to suck it up and get on with it. Rob said only half-jokingly once that he thought I had ventured onto the spectrum since becoming a parent as physical touch made me so visibly uncomfortable.

Who these lunatics are who are managing to have two babies with an eleven-month gap, or something equally insane, I'll never know. Like anything though, to each their own, and if you're managing to voluntarily touch your partner, let alone feel amorous, while you have small children, then good for you my friends. Enjoy all the sex. Have at it. Because the rest of us certainly aren't. I'm out here involuntarily recoiling if someone so much as accidentally brushes past me in Sainsbury's. I feel really mean sometimes because I can see that I've hurt Rob's feelings when I awkwardly untangle my fingers from his after he's tried to hold my hand for all of 17 seconds, but I just reach a point in the day when I can't be physically connected to someone or something anymore, and you shouldn't be expected to or feel guilty about that.

While I know we infantilise men a lot, they are fully capable of understanding your feelings if they want to. They don't have to get it entirely – unless they've been the one at home all day with children for weeks, months and years on end, then they probably won't ever get it – but there are basic levels of empathy that they're capable of if they're inclined to them. Like a lot of discussions we've had around different things with the girls since they were babies, I don't need Rob to understand what I'm saying necessarily, I just need him to accept it.

Managing Feelings

I've loved Rob throughout the whole process of having and raising the girls, and I've never questioned that, but there are definitely points when, as much as I love him and want to be everything that he needs and wants in a partner, sometimes I just don't have the mental energy to do any more emotional labour. I've managed the children's feelings and needs all day, and I don't have the capacity for his too.

It's really harsh written out in black and white, but everyone is ultimately responsible for their own feelings and we're grown-ups. Sometimes, you just have to suck it up and keep it moving for a while. This stage won't last forever – the trick is keeping it ticking over enough so that, when you do have the physical and mental capacity to make your partner's needs a priority, you still want to. Remembering how much you love each other while you're in the trenches of parenting is really hard on both physical and mental fronts. Maybe I'm exposing myself here, and other people will be reading this thinking, 'Nope, I've never felt more connected and as one with my partner', but I've had to remind myself I love Rob sometimes, and I do love him (before Rob reads this and starts pre-emptively contacting lawyers). If you're at the point of feeling so unbalanced in the scales of domestic labour where you really want to hurt your partner's feelings, though, then nothing I'm going to say here is going to help really. That's a much bigger conversation and one I'm probably not equipped to address.

It's so difficult when your time and energy is being pulled in a hundred different directions to remember to direct some of it at your partner. I think that's more the case for the default parents as well. It is not that the non-defaults aren't busy or stretched, because everyone has their own challenges in the day, but when you've spent a good proportion of the day without someone lying on you, been able to have an uninterrupted wee in peace and had the privilege of not trying to decipher eight different communication methods from school, it's easier to come home and have some headspace for your partner. Physically, right from pregnancy, nothing much changes for the dads either. My body has changed entirely, twice over, and it's hard to reconcile the new me with the old version in my head.

The Luxury of Privileged Ignorance

I'm probably going to make some non-defaults angry here, but I think it's fair to say that, at least anecdotally, a lot of people have partners who like to be babied a bit – men who, even before they became dads, leant into being looked after by their partner, who'd already tapped themselves out of house or domestic duties. Which is kind of fine before kids, because you have fewer demands on your time and, if what you want to do is look after your man, then have at it. No judgement here.

Pre-children, I took on most of the house things because, quite frankly, I cared more. I wanted it to look nice, and I was infinitely more bothered by how clean it was if people were coming over. That doesn't mean that you can just opt out of a fair division of domestic duties by claiming you don't care. Not to be almost painfully stereotypical here, but I've watched and feigned interest in many a football match (more at the beginning of our relationship admittedly) to show solidarity with Rob and what he cares about. I expect the same in return. Caring, or pretending to, about what your partner cares about is part of the deal.

The whole discussion is much less heightened when children aren't involved because you have more time and energy to deal with it. It's much easier to get over a grudge about cleaning the kitchen or sorting out the entire family's Christmas presents when you have some independent time to reset and forget about it. Once you have kids and you've done a thousand things for them already, as well as cleaned the kitchen multiple times because the children keep inconveniently insisting on being fed three meals a day, it's much harder to let it go when your partner also asks for something that they could so easily just do themselves. Like, is the dishwasher clean or dirty? Open it. What's in the fridge for dinner? I don't know, have a look. Where are my socks? They're not my socks, why would I know? What do I need to do for the weekend? I don't know, what are you planning on doing? It's very hard to maintain any level of patience, let alone tenderness, for a fully-grown adult who is adding to your burden.

If you're thinking 'weaponised incompetence' here, then 10 points for you. Most mums, or defaults of any flavour, don't get the luxury of being incompetent, let alone having the wherewithal to weaponise it. We're too busy googling how many times a baby should poo in a day or teaching ourselves the new way to do long division because the way we've been taught is apparently horrifyingly wrong to the youth of today. There isn't someone to ask a thousand and one quite frankly stupid questions to, so we have to figure this shit out and get it done. Maybe if I had my mum living with us I too could have the luxury of incompetence, weaponised or not, because I definitely still use her as my go-to font of all knowledge. While I'd like to offer an unreserved apology to my mum for every, quite frankly, stupid question I could have definitively worked out the answer to myself, she is my mum. And not my partner. Which is the difference here.

It's annoying enough answering the same question one hundred times to a ten-year-old. Or walking upstairs after being screeched at that their shoes are irretrievably definitely 100 per cent lost, only to discover that they are, in fact, the first thing you see, it's just much easier to sit on your tiny little bum and get your mum to walk up a flight of stairs and use her eyes, rather than your own. That's annoying, but they're children and you love them so you do some deep breaths, say some classic mum clichés that no one actually listens to, and move on. When it's your fully-grown adult partner, however, I want to murder someone. Rob mostly. With whatever ironically apt household item is to hand.

I'm not sure if I'd say 'weaponised incompetence' is appropriate really, as that implies at least a degree of intent, or purposeful selfishness, which I don't think most non-defaults are operating within. It's not incompetence, it's a privileged ignorance of the sheer quantity of things default parents have going on all the time – the physical domestic labour and mental load that defaults are constantly working through to keep everyone's trains running on the tracks successfully. It's not on purpose, but it's so ingrained that you're almost asking them to unpick their whole life's societal conditioning to be looked after, to be domestically directed, to be babied. Once you've got actual babies, however, they quite frankly need to grow up. And quickly.

Of course, NOT ALL MEN I hear you shout, or NOT ALL NON-DEFAULTS! Of *course* it's not all men or all non-defaults – lots and lots of non-defaults don't do this, and some defaults definitely do. Nothing is ever entirely black and white, but sometimes stereotypes are there for a reason and I don't think there are many defaults out there who wouldn't recognise at least some of what I'm saying to a degree.

Domestic Disparity

The crux of a lot of the discussions in the Beckett household is the argument about what's necessary and what isn't. Rob would argue that a lot of the work I do, I unnecessarily create for myself. While I agree that sticking individual rhinestones to a guitar for 18 hours because my daughter wanted a Taylor Swift guitar is probably not essential, the majority of my workload is necessary.

There are the basic things that have to happen for a house to function: laundry, cleaning, tidying, food shopping, and so on. No one would argue that they're optional really. Then there's the secondary list of 'necessary' things that might not be as elemental, but make everyone's life better: putting up seasonal decorations, sorting out drawers, helping with homework, organising birthday parties in advance, buying presents, booking haircuts, scheduling appointments, organising play dates, planning half-term activities, even the dreaded getting involved in school activities (fine, I will concede that this one I could happily kick to the kerb, but the girls like it when I go on their school trips so I suck it up, or send Rob on them whenever humanly possible) and the other innumerable things we do to keep everyone's lives fun *and* functioning – those thousand and one tasks that no one really notices are getting done, but they'd sure as hell miss if you stopped.

I've thought a lot about what would happen if I withdrew my labour, if I just didn't do what I was doing. How long would it take for the wheels to fall off, for no one to have what they needed for school or for all the birthday party options to be booked up? I would never do it because it wouldn't be me who suffered, it would be the girls – and I couldn't with a good conscience let that happen – but that doesn't mean that sometimes it's not really, really tempting.

Of course, there's the flip slide to this – the rebuttal that I know will be coming from Rob, which, really annoyingly, I don't think is entirely untrue: that he would do more but I don't let him. Which I'm loath to admit is probably a fair assessment. I could obviously let him do more, but that would require me to explain *what* needs to be done, but also try to justify *why* it needs doing and then *how* to do it as well. By the time I've given him the full rundown of exactly what, why and how, I might as well have done it myself.

I also don't let him do more because, quite frankly, he does it wrong. By wrong, I, of course, mean not how I would do it, which is obviously the unassailably correct way to do things now and forever and I shall brook no argument to this. It's hard to relinquish control of things that you're already doing, and have been doing for a long time. I'm thoroughly set in my ways and my routines, and I'm used to doing most of it by myself, not because Rob is lazy or uninterested but because I'm the default. It's also hard to let someone into a domain that you've had ownership over for so long, without any changes they might make feeling like criticisms.

It would be ridiculous if Rob and I were to split the domestic labour 50/50 as we are not splitting the labour of earning money 50/50. I am infinitely more available to do the school run because I'm here. I'm not expecting him to organise party bags after a five-show tour run, even though he would if I asked. Operating in counterfactuals isn't always productive, but I have often wondered, if the roles were reversed and I out-earned Rob and had gone back to work full time and he was more of the default parent, whether he would have taken on the breadth of tasks that I complete or whether he would have streamlined his duties into a more 'efficient' number, and I still would have ended up taking on the majority of responsibilities I have now.

Whatever your situation, whether you're back at work part time, full time or you've stayed off completely, I think it would be realistic to say that, in most households and partnerships, the domestic labour isn't split proportionally (women, for example, take on 60 per cent more household tasks than men[1]), even taking into account the other partner's working hours and responsibilities. By and large, it's the mums and women, or defaults, who are taking on the brunt of the mental and physical load of keeping a family functioning. If you're doubting this, then watch families on Christmas morning – there's almost always one adult there who is genuinely surprised when the presents are opened. Not only have they not wrapped a single thing, they haven't bought the majority of them either. Father Christmas is alive and well for many men out there because their partners essentially operate as a covert North Pole elf operative.

I can't square this circle, not for myself and certainly not for anyone else. I have the most supportive husband I know – one who actively volunteers when he can see me becoming overwhelmed (whether he's exasperated by the number of projects I've given myself or not). We have a work–life balance that is much easier on me than it could be had Rob's job been different. If my body could stop trying to poo itself to death whenever I get stressed, I could go back to work if I wanted to and we could organise childcare to facilitate that. (All of which would really test the mettle of Rob's resolve that 'I will do everything 50/50 with you if you want me to.') I know I'm very lucky to be in the position that I'm in.

I was speaking to a school mum who was telling me about her friend who out-earned her husband and they'd both gone back to work full time after having children. Despite both partners working full time, the weight of managing the household was still falling massively disproportionately on to her and it was causing real issues to the point where they were having counselling. It can feel impossibly fraught to try to bring up disparity in the familial workload when you've got kids, of any age, but especially when they're little and need so much physical intervention. It can feel like all you're doing is working and it's almost impossible not to get defensive when told by your partner that you're not doing enough. No one likes to be told that they're being lazy or not pulling their weight, even if that's quite clearly not what your partner's actually said. Default parents, women especially, don't have the luxury of being 'at capacity' when it comes to things their family or children need. They simply have to get it done.

It's so easy to work myself into an escalating tizz when I feel overwhelmed, and resentful about the perceived freedom that Rob has from the responsibility of being the default parent all the time. However, as much as I don't want and shouldn't have to ask, there's very little to be gained by being cross at him for not doing something that he has no idea exists. It's taken a long time to work out the logistics of how to navigate our roles as partners and parents, and, without alarming anyone at the start of the journey, we're 10 years in and still working out the kinks.

Lay it all out on the table, however works for you. For us, we do a 'domestic audit' to outline who's doing what and why for the next few weeks. We've never found it necessary, or even feasible, to list every task that needs doing, but what we have found useful is looking at our weeks and months ahead and working out where we can trade off things and carve out time for us individually and as a family. It's hard when you're on the treadmill of family life, which we know rarely stops for us to catch our breath, to identify where you have those opportunities, and not feel bad about it. I also admitted defeat and ordered some of those annoying smug TikTok mum whiteboards for the kitchen wall so I could put all the kids' information up somewhere everyone could see it. I add everything to a shared calendar. I also send Rob long voice notes and messages of what our Christmas plans are or what I'm organising for the kids' birthdays so I can always, *always* answer the inevitably stupid questions with 'I sent you that' or 'I don't know, check the wall.' Remove the margin of error and give them no quarter.

One for the non-defaults

If you're a dad or partner reading this and some of this is starting to sound uncomfortably familiar, and you're realising that perhaps, just perhaps, you're 100 per cent occupying the full non-default role, then do yourself a favour and make your long-term life easier right now. Look around you, use your eyeballs and see if there's something you could physically do to help. Go wild – open that dishwasher and see if it needs emptying *without* asking your partner. If we're really pushing the boat out, message the default in your life right now and say thank you. Don't wait until you're told to by the corporate greetings card industry or until your partner's had a meltdown over the never-ending list of jobs they have to complete. A little unprompted appreciation goes a long way in the trenches, I promise you. Most importantly, and I get this is more difficult to do, try not to assume. Don't assume your partner will do it. Don't assume your partner is coping just because everything is getting done and nothing's gone to shit yet – just because the pond surface is peaceful it doesn't mean the ducks aren't paddling furiously under the water, and the default in your life might just be at the absolute end of their reserves. And absolutely never, NEVER, make a joke or smirky comment about how hard they've worked that day or what they've done. All you're doing is making your partner feel disrespected and deflated. We are contending with enough guilt and default identity crises without you piping up with your throwaway little jokes.

If you are the default and, like me, don't know how to communicate that you don't appreciate these little 'jokes' about your life, there's some great expert advice coming up. This took me ages to learn, especially in the early days when who was most tired was a battle I felt deeply in my soul that I needed to win, but acknowledging what someone else is doing, or how hard someone else is working, doesn't negate how hard you're working. In teaching, we're told that positive reinforcement works better than punishment, carrot over stick wherever possible, and while I've lost sight of that a few times over the years when trying to talk to Rob about what we were each managing, life is nicer when you're nice. Help each other out and acknowledge the other's work. Ultimately, you'll get through the hard slog part of parenting, not necessarily quicker, but maybe that bit happier if you can remember you're on the same side. Babies, toddlers, kids – whatever stage you're at – it can feel like you're constantly tackling one battle after another, and you can't afford to let them divide and conquer you. You're on the same side and you need to remember that, if you're going to win the battles let alone the war, teamwork makes the dream work.

Romancing Your Roommate

This chapter is ostensibly about how to remember that you love your partner, and I've spent a lot of it talking about being teammates, which, I know, doesn't sound overtly romantic. I mean how many Hallmark movies do you see about people being really efficient teammates? Clintons isn't selling out of 'good hustle team' cards on 14 February each year. I'm not going to sit here and pretend that being teammates is full of hearts and flowers; however, it's the path back to romance. You're never going to get the time, space and wherewithal to feel romantically inclined to your partner if you're not on the same team. You might not have the same roles as each other, you might not be dividing the work evenly, but if you're going to get anywhere, then you have to be on the same side at least.

It's hard in the trenches of parenthood when you feel exhausted, underappreciated and hard done by to remember that, sometimes, you just need to acknowledge and recognise the other person's input. In what is an embarrassingly running theme, I just like to be told 'good job' sometimes. Rob recently did a whole load of therapy and, while most of what he now oh so Zenly says to me when I'm in the midst of whatever tizz I've got myself into makes me want to gouge my own eyes out, something he says that I think is really apt here is, 'What's in the way is the way.' Just like that bloody bear hunt you incessantly hear about as soon as you have children (thanks very much Michael Rosen), sometimes you just *have* to go through it.

There's no magic answer to being overworked and stretched too thin as a parent, and a partner. You just have to keep on keeping on, remaining as much of a team as you can, until it gets easier, because it will get easier. You slowly start to get little parcels of time back. You start to feel more like the person you were before you were pulled in a hundred different directions. You suddenly find a few spare brain cells to direct towards something other than which uniform is needed on a Thursday. So, just do what you need to do between then and now to stay on the same team. Whatever works for you – domestic audit or idiot-proof information sharing – you're a team and, like the SAS, you don't leave a man behind.

Ask the Expert: Anna Williamson

If it isn't already blindingly obvious, I'm not qualified in any capacity to give anyone relationship advice. Like anyone else, all I'm doing is my best and hoping that's good enough. So, instead of me imparting wildly ineffectual advice to just swear at your partner aggressively under your breath when they're not looking at you, I spoke to Anna Williamson, life coach extraordinaire, author of numerous mental health and parenting books, and resident relationships expert on *Celebs Go Dating,* to get some legit, actually helpful, expert insight and advice.

From speaking to my fellow defaults, there are reassuringly common themes in the frustrations we're experiencing with our partners – very rarely are we alone in our challenges, even if it can feel like it sometimes. What they boil down to is:

1. **Balance:** How can we balance our relationship and parenting more effectively?

2. **Communication:** How do we communicate effectively without causing an argument?

3. **Challenging traditional gender roles:** How do we work out how roles and chores should be divided in an ever-changing landscape?

4. **Identity:** How do we get back to feeling like us again after having children?

5. **Winning:** How do we win an argument with our partner?

So, below are the pearls of Anna's infinite wisdom, which hopefully will help you guide those conversations in a more productive, or at least less enraging, direction. I, an incessant yapper, interrupted her too much to print the whole interview verbatim, so I've summarised as best I can the advice and insight Anna imparted – which is probably more useful anyway when you're tired and need a quick reference point to get you out of an argumentative resentment spiral.

Balance: How can we balance our relationships and parenting more effectively?

Having a baby brings huge changes, and change is very hard for a lot of people. You need to be having clear conversations with each other about what you both want and need in this new landscape, otherwise that's when cracks can appear. You don't want those cracks to deepen into chasms just for lack of communication.

Parenting relationships are focused on role definition, and the earlier you address with your partner how you each see your parenting roles, the better. It's never too late to have these conversations, especially if one of you is unhappy with how your parenting landscape currently looks. Think about conversations like:

- **Role apportionment:** who's going to be responsible for what? You want to avoid 'chores wars' if you can.

- **Family values:** values and cultures can differ wildly between families and that's no bad thing, but you need to work out what each of you is expecting when starting a family and be prepared to accept compromises on both sides.

- **Going back to work:** who's going back to work? Is going back to work important to both of you? How much are you willing to sacrifice time at home or at work to have a family? Who is this going to fall on?

- **Childcare:** how do you feel about childcare? What ages? What settings? What balance are you happy with between childcare/being with parents in order to facilitate working?

A key point here is to have regular check-ins with your partner, with your family and with yourself, and to adjust, be flexible and compromise. Keep talking about the roles you're each occupying in your family as your family and lives will evolve and change, so those roles and chore apportionment can't be static either.

If going back to work is important to both of you, or financially necessary, then you're going to need to have frank and open discussions about what that will look like for *both* of you. Having a full-time job and being a full-time parent doesn't add up mathematically as they're two full-time jobs. To do both well is an enormous challenge, that might be impossible, and you have to consider, 'At what cost?' What's worth it for you won't necessarily be the same for your partner, so you need to be re-evaluating things together on a regular basis to make sure everything is balancing the best it can.

Communication: How do we communicate effectively without causing an argument?

When you're a parent, the absolute key thing, as we've seen, is constant, regular, open and effective communication with your partner. And that looks like – as best as you possibly can – not going on the attack. Typically, we only have these conversations when we're already cross, so try to pre-empt that as far as possible.

Don't wait until you're so far down the line that all your partner has to do is not put their Mars Bar wrapper in the bin and, suddenly, you're fucked off and ready for WAR. Recognise your triggers and bring it up EARLY, in a way that's not going to trigger arguments or escalate the situation.

The following tips will help you do this:

- Approach it from an 'I' perspective, which means always leading with how it's making you feel. It sounds 'woo-woo', but it's absolutely the best way to actually engage in productive conversation that doesn't result in an argument. If you come in with, 'You've done this and now I'm cross …' all the other person is hearing is an attack and then they'll feel the need to defend themselves because that's human nature. Reframe it in how it's making you feel: 'I'm feeling really knackered today and a bit pissed off, and I've just had to put this wrapper in the bin that isn't mine, and I'd really appreciate some support in this.' This is a far more productive way to approach the conversation that might result in them actually hearing and being receptive to what you're trying to say.

- If you can, try to avoid starting the conversation with, 'I don't want an argument but …' We're inadvertently planting the seed that, in fact, this will be an argument, as our brains can't receive negatives – we're not listening to the 'I don't want' part. All our brains are hearing is 'argument' and kicking into gear for one. Just don't plant the seed.

Relationships are fundamentally a partnership. We're one of the first generations that have chosen each other for love. Historically, relationships have been transactional – they were about procreating, societal gains, status, continuing bloodlines, and so on. Life has moved on, but only really a couple of generations ago. Both men and women can now equally choose our partners based on love, which comes with an expectation of balance and respect. This is where our relationship foundations come in: work out what you want your relationship and family to look like, no matter where you are on that journey. It's never too late. Spend some time thinking about it and then talk about what you want your future to look like and be open-minded to each other's ideas. Bear in mind the following:

- It's important to work out where you can compromise and where you can't. We never get what we want 100 per cent of the time, and nor should we, but what can you be flexible on and what are absolute deal breakers?

- It's hard when you're in the trenches of parenting to not slip into one-upmanship. When you're struggling, try to drill back down to what you love about your partner, what they bring to your life and why you wanted to do this in the first place.

Challenging traditional gender roles: How do we work out how roles and chores should be divided in an ever-changing landscape?

The challenge that we have as parents and partners is that we're being told now more than ever that everyone needs to be doing it all. It isn't just women's roles that have changed over the last few generations; men are being expected to do more in the family/domestic sphere than they ever have before. Historically, genetically and biologically, that's not how they've been expected to show up until this generation.

It's easy for us to bristle, especially as a feminist, that they 'should' be doing more, but, at the same time, it's much more productive to be open-minded about how we effect this change, so that the division of domestic labour is more equitable. I suggest:

- Finding a time, if you can, to sit down, when you're not both already cross, and talking honestly. Outline what needs to be done to run a home and a family. Discuss, and ideally agree on, what needs to be done and what's realistic in the set-up of the family dynamic of who's going to do what. When you're thinking about those roles, what could you do within your current set-up? What's the acceptable level of compromise here? Does this balance with what we need for the family to function?

- If it feels unbalanced for whatever reason, throw it out there as open questions: 'What can we do to make it more equal?', 'Is there a reason that I'm doing XYZ this week?' Open questions lead to discussions, and are much less likely to be received as an attack as it gives everyone the space to work out the answer themselves.

As women, especially as wives and mothers, there's an element of responsibility that we place on ourselves for the division of chores because we enable the imbalance. Check yourself on that:

- How much are you allowing it?
- How much are you assuming it's quicker and easier if you do it yourself?
- How much are you letting your partner actually do?
- If you're asking your partner to do something, are you giving them the space and freedom to complete those tasks?
- Are you expecting them to do it your way not theirs?

As with everything, communication and compromise are the key here. If you want things to change, you have to be open to the idea you need to change as well as your partner.

Identity: How do we get back to feeling like us again after having children?

I really missed my job because that was the only thing I knew I was good at, and I felt shit because I didn't know how to be a mum yet. Part of the healing process from postnatal depression was going back to work because I found my old identity and a bit of the old Anna again, which then, in turn, gave me more confidence in my parenting role.

The default parent is the mother, typically, especially if she's breastfeeding and she's recovering from birth. We continually underestimate the importance of that recovery time, the same as we underestimate the impact of giving birth and becoming a parent. But that time comes at odds with also having the time and space to nurture careers if we want to.

It's important to advocate for new parents. We've been able to minimise the impact of becoming parents to almost an acceptable running joke in society because everyone does it all the time. We need to not underplay to ourselves or anyone else the impact it has on the woman especially, but also both parents having to reconfigure their entire lives around this new person. Having a baby is great for everyone else, just not necessarily those two new parents in that moment. You are so detached from your life as you knew it in the space of 24 hours and we prepare ourselves as best we can, but no one can ever prepare you properly.

Struggling as a new parent is normal. Even if it feels like you're the only one, you're absolutely not. Work out what you need:

- Is that to go back to work and re-anchor yourself to your old identity?

- Is that to accept help from other people?

- Is that to stop breastfeeding?
- Is that for your partner to do more, even temporarily?

There isn't an easy answer here as it will be different for everyone. If someone could tell us the perfect equations of work–life–family balance, they would be a trillionaire. Once again, the key here is communication with your partner, and your friends and family.

Winning: How do we win an argument with our partner?

There is no other clever way for a relationship to come through conflict and resentment than just listening without judgement or reaction. You can't and won't solve anything without communication. We save up a lot of our frustrations and resentment and anger for our partner because we feel safest with their reaction, but just because we can, it doesn't mean it's helpful.

Of course, arguing isn't necessarily a bad thing. I'm more concerned about a couple in therapy that doesn't argue than does. Arguments show that you care and that you care about being heard and want to convey that to your partner. Arguing is human – the key is healthy arguing. Healthy arguing is making sure we don't throw shots that we can't take back. Words can hurt and you can't take them back once they're out there. Sometimes, you've got to leave and de-escalate, and come back to it when you've let the tension out and can actually have a productive conversation.

Bear in mind that everyone communicates in a different way; everyone handles conflict in a different way. The key is communication and compromise, both in what you're saying and how you're saying it.

Healthy communication and productive conversations aside, there's a lot of solace in standing behind the door giving them the double bird with as much ferocity as you can, swearing under your breath. Get it out cathartically.

7

CAN YOU HAVE IT ALL?

So, can you have it all? Short answer: no. Longer answer: yes, but it depends on what your 'all' is.

Before Germaine Greer appears on my doorstep to berate my lack of belief in women's abilities to do and have it all, that's not to say we *can't* have it all, but perhaps it isn't all it's cracked up to be. Maybe the physical and mental workload to have it all isn't what's best for us. Or the effort needed to have it all isn't worth the 'all' you're having.

As with *anything* I've already said so far, this is so deeply personal and everyone will have different versions of what 'having it all' looks like – of what's important to them and what they need to feel fulfilled, happy and whole. That's fine. What's right for you might not be right for me. Neither of us is wrong; we're just different. It's so hard not to be defensive over our own decisions when confronted with other people's different choices and outcomes because most of us are working the hardest we can to do the absolute best we can for our family and ourselves. It can feel like we have to defend our choices or achievements when we see someone else's – comparison is the thief of joy and all that jazz. I'm talking a very good talk here for someone literally seven chapters deep into what is quite probably a mental breakdown over my experience of becoming a mother, as it's so hard not to compare yourself to other people and what they're apparently managing to do.

The Good Old Days

We've never lived in a time when we've had access to so much. Back in ye good olde days, before formula and nurseries, we would have had to stay at home with our babies because if we weren't there to feed them, they'd die. We didn't know that Maureen from the other side of the world had birthed five babies, was running a full-time business and managing to be back in her size six jeans, because we only knew what the maybe ninety people in our village were doing. And they were all doing pretty much the same thing as us. Our brains had so much less to deal with. I'm not saying I'd like to go back to living in a cave waiting for a Neanderthal wielding a big stick to bring home a speared mammoth. However, maybe my particular brain could do with slightly less information about what everyone else is doing all the time. Would I feel so inadequate about what I've achieved since having small children if I didn't know what anyone else was managing?

I love social media – I know doomscrolling is bad for you, but I bloody love it and I refuse to give it up. I'd let China personally implant a data chip in my brain if it meant I could keep TikTok. But. BUT. There's no arguing with the correlation between my access to every gorgeously put-together mummy blogger under the sun and increasingly identifying as an uneducated, underachieving and unwashed foot. My tiny little pea brain hasn't evolved at the same rate as technology or modern society, and maybe I should come to accept that perhaps I should have been born in the Middle Ages when I could have better coped with the limited amount of information available to me at any given moment.

I don't actually want to live in the Middle Ages, of course; apart from anything else, they didn't have Coke Zero and I simply refuse to live in a time when I don't have access to a nice, crisp, sanity-saving can of deliciousness at any time of the day or night. The modern explosion of possibilities for women is and can only be a good thing. But, like Spider-Man, we need to remember that 'with great power comes great responsibility'. Just because we have the choice to do it all, it doesn't necessarily mean that we should, especially not at the same time; it's *so* much to try to have it all simultaneously. Looking at it logically, of course I'm not going to be the kind of partner, employee or friend I was before I was also a mother, because I've added to my plate. Even on those very rare days when I'm running at 100 per cent, I still only have 100 per cent to give. Forgive my terrible maths, but if I was using all my time and capabilities to be the best partner, employee and friend I could before children, then if I'm also now going to add being a halfway decent mum to that then that percentage to do so has to come from somewhere. There isn't more of me to utilise here. You're begging, borrowing and stealing from the rest of the components in your life to find enough bandwidth to work out how to suddenly be a mum as well, and ideally a good one at that. There's no more untapped capacity left to still give the same time and effort to all the things I did before, which is *normal*. We've got to learn to be kind to ourselves and, more importantly, realistic. The expectations we place on ourselves are insane when you really stop and look at it sensibly.

It's also backed up by the data: women are doing more than we ever have. Women spend on average 10 hours a week more than the men in their lives multitasking, with the majority of that time being spent on housework or childcare.[1] TEN HOURS. Think about what you could do with 10 extra hours! Ten hours of time when I'm not trying to split myself in two and do nine things at once? Yes please. These extra hours spent multitasking also lead to an increase in negative emotions, stress, psychological distress and work–family conflict.[2] So, next time you're told you're nagging or need to 'calm down', feel free to cite some scientifically collected data as to why exactly you're so much more stressed out than they are. You're welcome. If you need some more, a study out of America in 2024 found that mothers took on 7 out of 10 mental load tasks[3] – 70 PER CENT of the remembering, organising, anticipating, coordinating, doing; the 'cognitive labour' that goes into keeping a family functioning.[4] One more fun fact for you if you're in the throes of an argument and your non-default partner dares utter the words 'but you're just *better* at it than I am': men and women, as I'm shamelessly stereotyping the majority of defaults as women here, are as capable of multitasking as one another, as proved by a 2015 study.[5] This is not a gender difference. There is no innate reason why you as the default are better at it other than necessity and practice. So don't even try it non-defaults.

The Comparison Trap

There will always be someone who appears to be having it all with ease – and never more so when we look at the world of work. The relentlessness of the hashtag 'girlbosses' whenever you've opened social media in recent years really makes it feel like we should all be setting up viral companies while maintaining spotlessly aesthetic houses and also popping out suitably angelic-looking kids to boot. When you speak honestly with those people, though, it's never as idyllic as it maybe looks online or from the outside looking in. There will always be a compromise somewhere. Going back to work will almost always necessitate some level of childcare, and I would put money on you falling down a guilt spiral of doom because you've 'abandoned' your child and you're never around to do school pickups (even though this doesn't seem to bother the non-default parent quite so urgently, of course ...). Or so and so's mum at school who goes on every trip and is always at pickup with a healthy snack looking smug while you've chosen to go back to work full time. What a terrible mother! Or maybe you've gone back part time – the perfect compromise, right? Wrong! You probably feel like you're neither at home properly nor at work properly. Someone's always going to be managing to do better at work than you are because you're missing things while you're at home, while being told by the full timers how LUCKY you are to have all those days off to RELAX, when actually you're squashing a full-time parent role into two days, and also trying to keep up with full timers at work but in less time and for less money. Maybe you've decided to stay off completely and commit to being a full-time parent, but then, once you get a bit of physical distance from the newborn trenches, suddenly what you're doing isn't enough. You're wasting your life away drinking coffee. You're probably qualified or experienced in something. You were a whole functioning member of society pre-kids so WHY ARE YOU SO LAZY NOW? Of course, you're not lazy! Your work's just changed. But it's not enough. Your house should be spotless. You should be a size six with all this time to exercise. You should have set up a side hustle at home with all this mythical free time you've got, right? *RIGHT*?!

Of course, if you're managing to keep multiple trains running on their tracks successfully then more power to you. I'm proud of you. I'm proud of any default parent who's managing to keep shit moving, to be honest. I look on in awe at default parents who are fully defaulting, but also working, achieving, progressing. It's none of my business what compromises they're making to make it work for them, because it's working for them. For *them*. It doesn't need to work for me because they're not me, and we should all be keeping our noses out of other people's beeswax. Your decisions don't have to work for anyone else but you and your family. You just have to remember that everyone, no matter what it looks like, is making a compromise somewhere, even if it looks like they've got it 'all'.

What Is Your 'All'?

You absolutely can have it all; you just need to work out what your 'all' is. Short of a time machine, we're never going to be able to totally disassociate from the myriad possibilities of what we *could* be doing, because we have so much access to what everyone else is doing, saying, eating, wearing or working nowadays. The trick, not that I've successfully managed this so far, is trying to keep in your own lane. Try as much as possible to take the power of those inevitable comparisons away. Spend some time really giving yourself the space to look at your life and think for more than nine uninterrupted seconds about what you want, and what you need. For me, I need more than just being at home for Rob and the girls. I felt so incredibly spoilt for so long thinking, let alone saying, that it wasn't enough for me. On the flip side of that, however, nor did I want to return to full-time teaching because it simply took too much from me physically and would have taken me away from the life I've built at home as the default parent, mum and partner, which I do really love.

I want to still be at home. I want to be the girls' default. I just also want to do something that makes me 'me' again. I need something that's just mine and, instead of feeling bad about that, I'm trying to embrace just how normal that is. I want something to sink my teeth into. I want to feel challenged in a way that isn't persuading a 10-year-old to eat the accidentally purchased wrong brand of chicken dippers. I want my own group of work friends. I want stuff in the calendar that can't be rescheduled because it's 'work'. I want my stuff to be a priority as well. I've spent 10 years as the girls' mum and Rob's partner. It's OK to want my own stuff now as well. Of course, *of course*, if you're a default and stay-at-home parent and you're happy cracking on as you were, then keep on cracking my love. More than anywhere else in this book perhaps, to each their bloody own.

There are lots of factors at play when it comes to having it all. First and foremost, it takes time and some critical self-reflection to work out not what you *could* do, but what you *want* to do. Don't do something because you think you 'should'. Just because it might be physically just about possible to have a full-time job, run a beautiful home, raise well-rounded literate children and be the perfectly presented partner, it doesn't mean it's in any way necessarily healthy to try to attempt all of that simultaneously. There are very real practicalities to trying to 'have it all'. Start from the basis of what you need, and then what you want. If you need X amount of money for your lives to function, then work from there. If you want to be at home for X number of days with the kids, then work from that starting point. Whatever stage of children you're at, if you've been the default then you're starting on the back foot of prioritising your own needs again.

When I published my 'A Very Long Whinge' blog post (see louembeckett.co.uk), hundreds of people contacted me with their own stories and frustrations at the implications of being the default parent. What stood out were those messages from people who'd been defaults for decades, parents to fully-grown adults, still in that default role. The wistfulness was palpable; it wasn't that they'd not loved their partner, their children or the life they'd built. It was that time had passed and they'd never quite managed to break out of that default role and prioritise their own needs as well as their family's. That stayed with me. I love my life, I love Rob and, more than anything, I love being the girls' mum. But, more than that, I want to *keep* loving it. So, if what it takes for me to keep loving it is having the occasional bit of independence from it, then that feels like a sensible and fair swap really, doesn't it?

For me personally, having it all is a pipe dream – a mythical Ponzi scheme designed to keep everyone beavering away at the impossible. We simply aren't built to be *everything* to *everyone* all the time. That's an expectation put on defaults to contort ourselves into diametrically opposed beings simultaneously: a glass-ceiling-shattering boss at work, a nurturing Mother Nature at home and a siren to our partner. We're supposed to bounce back at the same time as not caring how we look because we're focusing so entirely on the babies. Loath as I am to quote the Barbie movie, but 'it's literally impossible to be a woman' sometimes. No one's expecting the men in this scenario to be all things to all people, 24/7, so why do we expect it of ourselves?

You've got to work out what's important to you right now. What can you manage in one go, without driving yourself mad? Maybe it's less about working out whether you can have it all, and instead working out what you can have *at the moment* at a cost that's acceptable to you. Part of the challenge of being a parent, especially a default parent, is that it's constantly evolving. Therein lies the challenge, but also the beauty. *Nothing is permanent.* Your children, and your role as their default parent, will change in a hundred different ways as time marches on, so, while it might seem impossible now, things will change. Wherever you are on your parenting journey, think about how much they've already changed from a few months or a few years ago. It can be hard to see how far you've come when you're in the thick of it, but you really have come so far.

Finding time to have it all

The 'leisure gap' is a fancy term for what we already all know: the non-defaults have more free time than the defaults. Well yeah, obviously. However, it's more than that. It's not just the disparity between the availability of time to participate in leisure activities or socialise, it's the feelings we have about our leisure time as well. It's hard to have time to work out what we want, or how we might achieve that, if we firstly don't get any time 'off' and, when we do, we waste that time feeling bad about it.

That the default parent, which, as we've established, is normally the mum in the majority of cases, has less 'free' time than the non-default is pretty much a given. The precedent is set so early on because the burden of growing, birthing and feeding a baby from conception throughout the entire newborn stage falls predominately on women. Physically, it takes time to recover from the enormity of pregnancy and birth, but breastfeeding necessitates our near-permanent proximity to the baby. If you're solely responsible for feeding a baby that needs feeding what feels like every 10 minutes in the first few months, then it's going to be physically incredibly difficult to get any real independent leisure time. That precedent continues – though the physical disparity between the roles of the mum and dad narrows as time goes on, the leisure gap doesn't. There's a really interesting study that I give you full permission to wheel out any time you want to win an argument, that men in America have, on average, half an hour more free time a day than women in America. Which doesn't sound like much, but, once you average it out and add it up, that's 164 hours a year. ONE HUNDRED AND SIXTY-FOUR HOURS. That's 6.8 24-hour days. If you work a 40-hour week, that's equivalent to more than 4 weeks' holiday.[6]

The leisure gap isn't just the time you have to spend doing things that keep you sane – it's the way defaults and non-defaults view their own free time. If you're the default, how many times have you been trying to relax or do something for you, and you've not been able to fully enjoy what you're doing because your old friend guilt makes an appearance? How many times are you interrupted by someone needing something? Or do you feel guilty for doing 'nothing' so you start doing something productive at the same time? You're not alone. The leisure time you spend as a mum/default is so much more fragmented than that of the non-default. You're six times more likely to feel stressed during leisure activities as a mum than a dad, which kind of defeats the point doesn't it?[7]

We're societally conditioned to be multitasking, to be doing it all, to be always on top of things, and we can feel insanely guilty when we're not doing that, when we're prioritising our own well-being. Generally speaking, the non-defaults don't – and that, more than 'having it all', is what I think is more important here.

It's all about rebalancing that approach to 'free time'. You're much more likely to be in a position to have it all, or at least however much of it you actually want, if you're not tying yourself in knots feeling guilty about things you have no business feeling bad about. Sitting down to watch a *Real Housewives of Beverly Hills* marathon after you've got everyone up and out for the day with everything they need? Nothing to feel bad about there. Taking some time to exercise? That can only be a good thing. We've got to take a leaf out of our partner's books and lean into the non-default mindset – that we don't always have to be 'on'. We don't always have to be doing something 'worthwhile' for it to be worthwhile. Recharging your batteries and making sure you're not pouring from an empty cup *is* worthwhile in and of itself. Just because you can't quantify it, it doesn't mean that it isn't beneficial.

That translates over into childcare as well as leisure time. If you split childcare responsibilities into four main categories – physical, managerial, educational and recreational – in three out of the four categories women, mums, dare I say it, the defaults, are doing almost double the amount of work than the dads. The only childcare activity where the labour is pretty equitable is recreation.[8] The fun stuff – playing, fun activities, days out. It's much easier to be relaxed and not stressed if the primary childcare labour you're doing is fun. Everyone can be fun at the park, but come back to me on hour three of fruitlessly trying to make an eight-year-old do comprehension homework on women in space and let's see how stressed you are then matey-boy.

So, how do you get from where you currently are – multitasking, organising play dates, emptying the dishwasher, loading the washing machine, fielding emails from school, keeping up with friendships, helping with homework, trying to do your 10,000 steps round the living room while also watching your programme and 'relaxing' – to the point where you can actually enjoy your leisure time? Firstly, like so much of the advice before, talk to your partner. You're not going to relax if you're being interrupted. It's not leisure time if you're also doing domestic labour at the same time. Lean into being selfish. Even though it's not selfish, sit with that feeling of being selfish. Sit with the guilt. Let it work its way through you. Let it get into perspective. And then let it pass. You're not going to stop feeling guilty about taking the time and space you need to do whatever it is you want to be doing if you constantly try to assuage the guilt by compensating for that time elsewhere. Sometimes, the only way through is literally through. Feel guilty. Feel bad. Feel lazy. But do it anyway. We're trying to undo years and years of learnt behaviour here, from both sides. Yes, of course, in an ideal world, your partner would go, 'Darling! I've realised I'm taking on far less of the mental and physical load here, and you simply must have some time to yourself! No, don't prepare anything before you leave the house! I don't need a list! I'm a competent grown adult, I can cope.' But we all know that it's not going to happen spontaneously because the non-default is having a bloody lovely time and no one's ever told them differently; why would they change such a beneficial (to them) status quo that they probably don't even realise exists?

Both you and your partner have to embrace the change, and if they don't understand it then fine, but they should be willing to accommodate your needs as well as their own once you've expressed them. It's going back to that privileged ignorance that we spoke about in the last chapter – we've been told *forever* that men can't multitask, and it's got to the point where it's almost treated as funny: 'Oh, aren't they silly – they can't do two things at once, bless them.' No, not bless them. If I can manage homework, answer emails and sort the school bags for tomorrow then so can you.

There's that phrase they use a lot in schools, especially to girls – that you can't be what you don't see. So, in the same way we show little girls that the world is their oyster irrespective of what career field they choose to go into, sometimes we need to show our partners what we need. Let's shine a light on the shadowy areas of default parenting and even out the playing field a bit. I really want to watch American middle-aged women with faces that don't move screaming at each other uninterrupted by domestic thoughts, and I promise I'll be a better mum for it.

Peer Pressure

At least some of this pressure to 'have it all' is coming at us from others. The pressure to be a brilliant parent, to have a solid relationship, to be working in a fulfilling and successful career, is coming as much from the outside as from within. Almost as soon as you get pregnant, you're met with an absolute avalanche of other people's opinions, choices, judgements, approvals and disapprovals. You can't do wrong for doing right. You don't need to spend very long on the internet before you see someone dragging someone else through the hedges for something they disagree with. And when it comes to women, and the choices women make, it's a weird and, quite frankly, embarrassing quirk of the system that it seems to be mostly other women who have the biggest issues. Obviously, with pregnancy, children, parenting, motherhood and everything that comes with it, for all the thousand and one reasons I've already waffled on about, it's a woman's domain mostly, so it's understandable that we're more interested or invested sometimes.

Even so, the fervour with which some people respond to other people's decisions, in a lot of instances, perfect strangers with obscure usernames, on the internet is still pretty shocking. Parenting is *so* hard and takes so much from us in every capacity – especially if you're actually trying to do it well – that I get how seeing someone else doing it differently *could* feel like an attack. It's so incredibly easy to jump into defensive mode when you feel like the hardest work you've ever done and the most difficult decisions you've had to make are being questioned by other people doing it differently. Can I suggest, however, that we all just take a bloody breath and give ourselves a beat to think about whether maybe now is a good time to be seen and not heard?

Parenthood, especially as the default, is so hard and we routinely underestimate the enormity of it because it's so widespread. We minimise the impact that becoming a parent has on us because if we thought about it to its fullest totality, we'd probably all go a bit mad and no one would ever have any children. Just because it's widespread and normalised, however, doesn't mean that it doesn't have a huge impact on the individual involved. In that context, when everything you've known before is forever changed, it's easy to see how your reaction to things might become slightly skewed. Because our lives as the parent, or as the default, are so impacted by the changes that children and family life bring, we have to justify to ourselves and other people just how hard it is, but also just how much we're achieving. Just how well we're doing it – the work and sacrifice worn almost as a badge of honour; undeniable proof that you're working the hardest, that you've sacrificed the most, that your achievements are worth more than someone else's because yours are harder won.

We're all so ready to detract from another mother's achievements in order to make our own feel bigger and it's really sad. It's been a solid three decades since the Spice Girls told us to spice up our lives and we're still not all on board the girl power bus. What would Scary Spice say if she could see us hey? Get with it girls – we're on the same bloody team people. You went back to work straight away? Lovely. You stayed off for decades catering to your child's every whim? Also lovely. Good for you. Good for me. Good for all of us. I literally don't care what you did as long as you were happy with it. It's none of my business what you did or why, as long as it worked for you. There's enough parent guilt to go around without us adding to each other's. It's a zero-sum game if you make yourself feel better by making someone else feel worse. I say to the girls a lot that you don't make yourself feel big by making someone else feel small, but they're children; we shouldn't have to say it to grown adults.

The biggest bit of advice I can give you here is, with none too little irony in this contradiction, don't look for advice, reassurance or validation from strangers – whether that's smug parents at the school gate or anonymous posters on parenting forums. Instead, curate yourself a group of people whose opinions you value and judgement you trust, and talk to them. That could be family, chosen or otherwise, that could be old friends, that could be the sanest mum at your baby group – whoever. The best advice that actually helps you feel better, which has a positive impact, is going to be from the people who know you and care about your well-being, not those lunatics at the school gate or on the internet who need to prove something to themselves by showing everyone how much harder they're working than everyone else.

There is no easy way out as a parent, just different ways to do things depending on what works for you and feels right *for you*. Your easy choice is someone else's hard one and vice versa. If there was one supreme way of doing things then Waterstones wouldn't have approximately 3,987,329,487,102, 398,120,938,265 books on birth, parenting, pregnancy, weaning, toilet training, behaviour management and, quite frankly, Grealish knows what else.

Ultimately, you do you babe. It's hard enough without anyone else chiming in. You're a competent adult. Back yourself.

Friendships

It's a real oxymoron of having babies that when, more than ever, you need a really solid group of women around you to keep you sane, you're going to probably be the worst friend you've ever been – especially to friends who knew you pre-baby. There's absolutely no getting around it – your friendships will shift and evolve, and it's not a bad thing, just something to be aware of and prepare for. I wasn't at all and I've made some fuck-ups because of that.

I was the first out of all my groups of friends to have a baby, and it impacted me in ways I wasn't prepared for. I physically wasn't as available as I was before children – seeing them took so much more logistical preparation and it started to chip away at the time I spent with them. That didn't mean I loved them any less. My uni girls, for example, have been the bedrock of the past 20 years of my life. I've known them longer than I've not known them and they're part of me – I just don't have as much of me to give anymore because being the girls' mum is taking so much of my time and headspace, and that's been a process of adjustment I struggled with.

It's hard not to feel like you're missing out when you're the outlier. Of course, we did things where I could bring the baby, and they were all so generous and travelled to see me quite a lot. Geographically, we cover the breadth of the UK and, in spite of that, they were still all sitting in my flat within a couple of weeks of me giving birth, supporting me and loving on her.

What I didn't really prepare myself for once I'd had our eldest is that I just didn't have what I had before to give to friendships. Not just physically – though the logistics of trying to socialise with a small potato is definitely a hurdle – but where I was so addled by trying to keep a small human alive and myself sane, I felt like I was constantly missing messages or forgetting things. I'd be so out of the loop with what was going on with my friends because I couldn't see beyond what was happening to me right then. They all got it and no one ever once made me feel bad, but I wasn't, and couldn't be, the kind of friend I wanted to be or was used to being.

What I've learnt in the 10 years since having our eldest is that the best kind of friends you could have, and the best kind of friend you can be in return, is one who will meet you where you're at. Who will give you the grace to only give what you can and not berate you for it.

Friendships will change as your lives change and what you had to give at 17 or 22, or 30 even, isn't necessarily what you have to give at 35 or 40 when you have the demands of a career, children or a family. And that's OK. I've had to lose some friends along the way who couldn't or wouldn't accept me for what I had to offer. And sometimes what I had to offer was pretty dismal if I'm honest with myself. Properly good-egg friends who are worth the time and effort will never berate you for doing the best you can, though, even if that's shit. Because you won't be shit forever.

If I could venture some advice here: as someone who has felt like they're failing at everything, in being a good mum, in being a good partner and definitely in being a good friend, it's to not overstretch yourself. I know, trust me, I KNOW you want to be the same kind of friend you were pre-baby, and that will definitely come back, but you need the bandwidth to do it. I'd like to be the person always making the most effort, who remembers important dates (and I do try – but now I have to save them in my phone and set multiple alarms so I don't forget), who is always there, answers every message and picks up when someone calls. Instead, I'm the person who realises in horror that I've not replied to a message three days/weeks/months later and then has to apologise for being terrible before the conversation can carry on. After a good few years of feeling like I was constantly disappointing people no matter how hard I tried to please everyone, I realised that I could no longer be all things to all people because there simply isn't enough of me or hours in the day to go around.

Something's gotta give. I've learnt to under-promise. I'd rather say no, and then say yes later if Rob isn't working, than have to cancel plans I've agreed to. I overcommitted myself for years trying to still be the person and friend I was before kids, but it was impossible. At least it was for me. I'm lucky enough to have the best of friends who include me in everything, even when I can't go; who I know will always be there for me, no matter how much I feel like I'm failing them. If your friends are making your life harder at a time when it's already hard, then maybe they're not the friends you need right now.

So, Can You Have It All?

Ultimately, what I've come to realise is that, for me at least, it's impossible to have and do it all, especially at the same time. As old Newton said, everything has an equal and opposite reaction. What goes up must come down. If you put into something, then you have less to put into something else. What I'm trying to be better at is working out what I need now, and not comparing that to where I was 10 years ago because that person's gone, and also not to worry about what might be happening in another 10 years' time because that person's not here yet. Things can and will change and evolve as the kids get older and, while it seems interminable now, it isn't permanent. Your friendships, your relationship, the children's needs and your identity in relation to all of those things will constantly evolve over the years, so just roll with the punches as best you can, but know it's not forever.

The most important thing for me right now is to be honest with myself about what I need and want, and for me to be honest with Rob about that as well. There's no point being cross or complaining if I'm not taking some ownership of the situation and communicating to him what I need. What I've needed in the past year or so is something that's mine, something beyond being a parent. I didn't want to not be the default parent, but I needed something else as well as that. The challenge has been in working out what that 'else' could look like. What's also challenging is allowing yourself to both feel that need for more and lean into it without tying yourself into guilt-ridden knots that being a parent isn't 'enough'.

Give yourself some grace that being the default parent is incredibly hard and you can only stretch yourself so thin before you snap. You don't have to do it all or at the same time as anyone else. There's no point in having it all if you're so mentally and physically exhausted that you're not enjoying any of it because of this quest to be the ultimate everything parent.

So, can you have it all? Yes, but where's the fun in that?

The Cheat Sheet of the Overwhelmed

Call me a Petty Betty, but sometimes I just need to feel vindicated, and quickly. Most of the time, I can breathe and let it go, but sometimes I. Just. Need. To. Know. I'm. Not. Going. Mad. This is where this page is going to come in handy …

It's all well and good peppering stats and data through this book, but in the midst of a rage spiral or being totally overwhelmed, sometimes you just need a quick reference point that's easy to find without having to trawl through pages and pages, and here it is! Use, abuse and cite these stats as and when you need to, or just have a read through whenever you want to feel vindicated that, yes, you are the most tired and, yes, you definitely are doing the most work.

- **You are definitely doing more – the UK government agrees with you!** 'Irrespective of their working time, mothers spent a significantly larger amount of time caring than fathers on weekdays.'[9]

- **Your brain *is* juggling more!** Mothers are doing 70 per cent of the mental load.[10]

- **You're absolutely right – the house would fall apart without you.** Women spend 10 extra hours a week multitasking household tasks compared to men.[11]

- **Give no quarter and accept no excuses!** Men and women are just as capable of multitasking as each other.[12]

- **You don't have the same amount of free time and you're right, it's *not* fair.** Men have half an hour extra 'free' time a day on average – that's 164 hours a year.[13]

- **It's perfectly rational to be stressed out – you're not being unreasonable, your leisure time is constantly interrupted.** You're six times more likely to be stressed than your partner in your leisure time.[14]

- **You're not nagging – you just don't get the luxury of being the fun one all the time.** Mothers are doing almost double the amount of childcare in every area apart from the fun parts.[15]

- **You *are* more tired.** Women lose 40 minutes of sleep per night after a baby; men only lose 13![16]

- **You're not an irrational rage-filled harpy – you're just tired!** Poor sleep leads to conflict in romantic relationships, so your partner needs to let you sleep![17]

8

ROB'S RIGHT OF REPLY

(FROM BEHIND ENEMY LINES)

In a massive reversal of roles, Rob's been featured heavily so far as an up-until-now entirely silent entity. For once, I've been in charge of the narrative, and it's been his turn to be unceremoniously thrown under the parenting bus. Jokes aside, I thought it was only fair to give Rob his say here, but also it'd be interesting to explore his perspective as the counterpart to my defaultness – as the parent who is so thoroughly occupying the non-default role in our dynamic. I was intrigued to see what those roles mean to each of us and how we've experienced the wildly different facets of ostensibly the same parenting journey. I've attempted (key word here: attempted) to speak to Rob the parent and husband, and not Rob the comedian. So, while he simply cannot help himself sometimes, I think we actually got some semi-serious thoughts from him for once. He really did try his very best to keep his showing off to an absolute minimum. How successful he was at that, I'll leave to your judgement.

Do you feel like we made a plan about who would do what once we became parents?

Rob: There was absolutely zero plan said out loud. I think it was just an unspoken thing that I would be in charge of getting the money that we needed, while you focused on getting healthy and growing a baby. You did say you would be in charge of all the paperwork and filing it, but that box full of paper is still in the loft untouched …

You made a lot of sacrifices in regard to your own career and also your own social life because of what I was doing. I would literally pick up the phone and go, 'I've been offered to do this. I've got to go there.' So, I think our entire life was very like kick bollock scramble, as I like to call it, where it was just like chaos. We didn't talk about it, but I was like, 'Well, Lou will pick up the slack with the kids and be the main default parent because if we're carrying on the way we have been, I'm just going to be going off and my career is taking priority because it's bringing in quite good money and there's loads of sort of life-changing opportunities coming our way if it goes to plan.'

Lou: *I think talking about a plan wouldn't necessarily have changed what we did, but, in hindsight, maybe it would have made it easier for me to process the fairly sudden change in my identity. I've always liked a plan, a cohesive set of instructions to follow, and if we'd spoken about what we were going to do and why, I think I might possibly have had an easier time processing what I was going through because I could chalk it up to stage one of the plan, with part of the eventual plan being a re-evaluation of our roles and careers later down the line. Who knows though? Maybe I would have always lost my marbles.*

Did parenting surprise you?

Rob: I couldn't believe how tiring it was. People tell you that you will be tired, but I've never known anything like it. It starts with emotional exhaustion at the birth, then it turns into physical exhaustion for five or six years, then it goes back to emotional exhaustion that, from what I see in older parents, carries on until you die.

Lou: *Hard agree. It's relentless; you just never catch up. Even if you're blessed with family or friends who will have your* *little cherubs overnight, there's no way to recoup the lost sleep, time and energy from having children – you're constantly living in a deficit. Which you do get used to, or you just get more OK with running at 50 per cent of your previous physical and mental capacity.*

When I use the term 'default parent', what do you think it means and what's your definition?

Rob: The parent that does more of the unseen legwork of being a parent. The main logistics and admin of everything.

Lou: *I was going to ask Rob to define what he meant by 'logistics and admin of everything' but it felt like a trap, because there's no way to properly list out everything a default does without losing your marbles, but I would kind of like to see him try.*

Are you the kind of dad you thought you were going to be?

Rob: I thought I would be able to sort out everyone's problems, and that would be my main job as a dad and a partner, but I've realised that you've got to allow your children space to sort their own problems so they gain confidence and independence. Same with you – you needed to find yourself again after having kids. I couldn't do it for you – I could only support and facilitate what you needed. Like making sure you get enough time away from the kids to actually be able to work, etc. Or just drink more coffee and do Pilates with your mates.

What's your main memory from the baby or toddler years?

Rob: I will be totally honest that I found the first couple of years an absolute blur; I can't really remember any of it. I have flashbacks, like getting our eldest to have the non-dairy formula when she refused to drink it.

I remember being so heartbroken watching you try to breastfeed and the toll that it was taking on your body and mind when you couldn't.

I remember being able to get our youngest to sleep really well by bobbing her about. But I was in such an anxious and fearful headspace at that point that I can't remember much of the early stuff for either of the girls. Mainly fear to be honest, constant fear, but when Covid hit and I had to be at home more, I started therapy and the fog started to lift so I have more memories from when the girls are a bit older.

As the non-default, do you feel left out of the loop at all now or are you happy with your role?

Rob: I felt left out sort of immediately from the pregnancy because you were obviously going through something physically and emotionally whereas nothing changed for me. Once we conceived, I was just hanging around till the baby came. Also, with hormones and things, I never really knew what the right thing to do or say was, and I'm never going to understand or feel what you're going through by carrying a baby and having to give birth. So there's an immediate sort of biological barrier of 'Well I'm not involved in any of this really.'

Even when they were a bit older, I remember I used to go away for a few days working and then I would come home and offer to put the kids to bed, but the way kids change so fast, I'd be doing the normal routine that has always worked and then you'd pop up as the parent who's been there and say, 'Oh, that doesn't work anymore', and then for me it's like, 'Oh God, when did that change?' So then two things happen. One: I feel useless. Two: I get defensive and feel embarrassed that I can't do it anymore. Then you lose your confidence. So then I'd be saying, 'Well, you do it then' when all you need is for me to do it and give you a break.

If I am brutally honest, I love being the non-default. It's really liberating having no idea what's going on. I feel like a courier – I just get a list of names and locations and times, and I'm off out the house doing my jobs.

Though sometimes I know it works the other way where some people do it bad on purpose. So that they can go, 'Oh, you're better at this than me' and take the piss. The same way as my dad always used to get me to make him a cup of tea when I was a kid and I used to make it badly on purpose so he wouldn't ask again.

Lou: *So what Rob's saying here is he started his weaponised incompetence as a man really early … Good to know.*

Is there anything you feel like you can't do that I can or vice versa when it comes to parenting?

Rob: I feel like I offer nothing if they have any problems with their bits. Everything else I can make a guess at. But I don't have a vagina. I hand those questions and problems straight over to you. I feel like I should do some research about puberty for girls and periods and things like that, as I want to be able to offer support and help in an educated and mature way. Rather than thinking I'm being gentlemanly by sticking my head in the sand.

I also can't help them with homework because of my dyslexia, which does make me feel quite ashamed and embarrassed, so you are the go-to person for that. Lisa the babysitter takes a few stray homework bullets too.

I am in awe of how amazing you are around special occasions and birthdays. You go to such a great effort for the girls and they love it so much. I feel like I'm not the best at celebrations and stuff like that.

I feel that maybe because I'm not at home as much as you are, and you're with them most of the time, sometimes they open up to me more than you about things. I think that's mainly because I spend more time with them doing fun things, or relaxing in our downtime. Whereas you are doing more of the logistics and getting them ready for stuff so there's a lot of rushing about and you telling them what to do, so there's not as much time to discuss things like there is with me sometimes. It's much easier to chat about worries on a Saturday chilling on the sofa than in the middle of a, dare I say it, quite fraught and emotionally charged hair brushing before the school run.

Lou: *That's fair, and goes back to some of the research I found about dads/non-defaults spending the majority of their childcare time in 'recreation' activities rather than logistical. It's the blessing and curse of being there more I suppose. I spend lots of time with them, which is lovely and precious, and all that jazz, but a lot of the time I spend with them is me telling them to do things. Get ready. Clean their teeth. Eat their dinner. Get in the car. Do their homework. Tidy their room. It's logistics. Which is boring anyway, but logistics with small children is both boring but also fraught as they just don't listen, so you inevitably have to nag. They're bored of me. Bored of my voice. Bored of being asked to do things. I'm bored of me to be honest, and I AM ME.*

When Rob's home, they're not bored of him, so they gravitate towards him because it is so much easier to be the fun, relaxed one if you haven't had to do the logistics side. It's not fair really that Rob's always the returning hero, but I'm playing the long game. It took me until I had my own children to properly appreciate just how bloody hard my mum must have worked when my sisters and I were growing up, as my dad worked long hours in the week so very much got all the glory at the weekends. We're really close as a family even now and I hope I manage to do the same with the girls when they're grown up. As long as they're talking to someone, I don't mind if Rob's their calm safe space at the moment, as long as they're happy.

How important were new parenting friendships to you?

Rob: I wanted them so you would have support in the local area when I was away. But, for me, I wasn't that bothered at all. However, we did meet some lovely couples at the antenatal classes who were great fun to be with. Big up Nic and Duncan. As the girls have grown up, I think it's important for them to have children around that are a similar age that they enjoy playing with. But I quite liked and still like just being together as a four. I am from such a massive family that I found fun but quite overwhelming at times – we would meet up for a picnic at the beach and there would be 50–80 people there. So I am enjoying the small unit of a four as it's a novelty and easier to navigate days out and restaurants. I also think it allows you time to all properly connect with each other about feelings and what everyone wants to do, rather than being swept up in a crazy gang.

Do you think you need to be as involved with the girls' school and friends as I am?

Rob: I feel like you're better at that kind of thing, maybe because I do so much socialising and talking to people at work that I'm kind of tapped out by the time I get to school stuff. You're better at knowing who everyone is and I do appreciate that it's quite important because then you know who everyone's kids are and who's doing what. It feels like I've gone in my head, 'Lou sorts that out' the same way as when I go on a tour, there's someone at my office that does all my train tickets so I've boxed that off as done, because someone else is doing it. And the same way within our relationship, I feel like

I've boxed off who's in charge of like logistics for the kids' schools, of what they're wearing and what they're doing, and that's you. My role is going out to work and sorting that side of everything out, or at least it has been for a long time. I think we're in a real transition phase now though where we're rebalancing everything, so it's exciting.

Did you ever feel like an imposter becoming a dad?

Rob: Not really, I found it tough, of course, but I always wanted to be a dad and I felt so lucky and privileged for it to happen.

I had no idea what I was doing really, but it's hard to feel like an imposter because so many of the stereotypical 'dad' behaviours I saw as a child weren't great if I'm honest and I really wanted to be different to what I'd seen. So I worked really hard at doing more and being more involved than a lot of the stereotypical dads from my childhood. From my background, the women did all of the childcare and the dads went to work. When the dads did anything wrong, it was laughed off as 'silly Dad packed the wrong swimming clothes and no towel'. So there was no pressure on dads to get it right. Whereas if one of the women had packed the wrong swimming stuff, she would have been scolded as a bad mum that doesn't know what she's doing. So I didn't have an ideal to live up to as such. It wasn't an imposter syndrome really – it was more an identity shift rather than being an imposter.

I felt and still feel a lot of the time like I'm almost cosplaying my own life as 'Mum'. I was curious whether you felt like that too?

Rob: This is a slightly deeper answer and not so much to do with losing my identity once becoming a parent, but more that I feel like I lost my identity slightly as soon as I became recognisable, like I didn't belong entirely to myself anymore. When I come home, I don't want to be Rob Beckett, I want to be Dad, so I'm really happy to lean into that role when I'm home.

Also, because having children didn't really impact me as such from a work perspective, I never lost that identity, just added 'parent' to it. I remember doing *Taskmaster* six days after you having the baby. It's sort of two things: one is that it's great in a way that you don't lose your identity. It was immediately, 'Oh, come back to work then cos you're a bloke and you didn't give birth' so everyone expects you to just crack on and you can totally just crack on. There's no physical need for you not to be able to jump straight back into work.

But, on the flip side, there's almost zero thought that you might be quite emotional and vulnerable. That you're having to leave this new baby at home and go straight back to work.

Even now, people ask me about work before they ask about the kids really, do you know what I mean? Being a dad, especially at the beginning, was seen as secondary to who I was as a comedian by a lot of people, so I didn't really struggle with losing my identity as such. So, when people see me, it's always, 'How's work?' and then, 'Oh, how's Lou getting on with the kids?' But they wouldn't be like, 'How are you getting on with the kids?' or 'How are the kids?'

Lou: *That's interesting, because I have the opposite I think – the combined impact of your career really taking off and having our eldest I felt like my identity almost completely disappeared overnight. People would ask me about you, or about the baby, it was so rarely about what I was doing because I wasn't doing anything else really was I? I was a mum and I was your partner, and that really impacted me, more than we realised I think. So, whereas you almost became more and more your identity since having children, that was running almost perfectly counter to me becoming less of mine.*

Do you have to find time for you?

Rob: When they were really little, when I came home, I felt like I was clocking into another shift of work. Where it's not 'Oh, I'm at home to chill,' it's 'Right, I've got to help now with the baby.' So if I was getting a train up to Manchester and just sitting down for three hours, it was like going on a mini break. You sat down and you got a coffee, you read your book. Which you, as the default parent, didn't get.

I could be away for work and I'd get to have a little drink, or say I finished work at 3pm and I told you I'd be home at 6, I could go, 'Oh, I'll have a little drink because actually Lou's not expecting me until 6pm anyway.'

I think I was fairly good that I didn't take the piss that much with it. I know for a fact there are some parents and, when I say parents, I mean dads, that will absolutely take the piss.

Especially now that they're older and a bit less labour-intensive, I would say that I'd rather be at home with them than sat in Darlington by myself all day waiting to do a tour show. It's hard to complain because, yes, I've had a break from being in charge of children, but I don't think it counts as 'me time'.

How has our relationship changed since becoming parents?

Rob: When we first had our eldest I think you probably had postnatal depression and, at the same time, I was suffering from anxiety and low-level depression. I ended up having a mini breakdown in 2020 when we had a 4-year-old and a 2-year-old where it all got too much. But we have become so much better at communicating over the years and I think we understand each other and can support each other so well. Since the girls have been at school, I feel like we are finding the time and energy to be silly and fun again.

We've been on this mini roller coaster of you finding yourself again, which is what's led to this book, but when we first had kids it was very rocky. Not our relationship, as I was always there for you and you were always there for me, but I feel like, back then, we were at the start of a 100-metre race with our heads down and ploughing through the hard work years of having small babies, whereas we're in a different phase of our life now where we're hitting our stride a bit. I feel like I broke into that stride a little bit before you as well because you lost all of your identity and who you were early on when we had the girls whereas I carried on working at least. That probably hit harder for you, especially because of who I am and what I do, because I'm very much in a public sphere so people will ask you about me instead of asking about you.

From the non-default parent perspective, how did reading my blog post make you feel? Did you realise I felt like that?

Rob: Who said I'm not the default?! No, I'm joking. I think I knew deep down that you were frustrated, but also that you felt guilty because we have a nice life and there was no immediate need for you to return to work for financial reasons. So you felt frustrated, slightly spoilt, you had mum guilt but were also low in confidence. You were fulfilled as a mother but unfulfilled as an individual. I could see something was wrong, but you hadn't really expressed that properly to me, but I knew it was something I couldn't help with. So I stood back and let you work it out. I believe everyone is on their own life journey and, as much as I love you and would do anything for you, I couldn't solve your problems – only you could.

I was really glad you wrote it out because I think I express myself verbally and you express yourself through the written word.

I was really happy and proud that you'd told me how you were feeling about being the default parent, and not just that, but you'd also done it in a public way. I was very happy that I could read what you'd written and go, 'Oh, so that's what the problem is' kind of thing.

Because looking back there was a period where I worked every day essentially and you were at home every day. It worked in the long term because that was only for a couple of years and now we have opportunities and things we can do because of that focus on my work, but now we need to try and make time for you to go and do you a bit more.

Do you think our balance between 'default' and 'non-default' roles has changed at all from newborn to toddler to school age?

Rob: I want to do as much as possible with the kids, but our situation is unique as we have no schedule or plan. My work is so erratic and last minute that it's always changing and you kind of have to roll with it. The only constant we have at the moment is that you have to pick up the slack with the kids because I'm at work. Without loads of childcare, that we couldn't have afforded at the beginning anyway, there wasn't really another way to do it that made sense with the kids and your health. But it does make it hard to even out the load more because there's no long-term consistency to anything I do. Sometimes, we'd need a full-time nanny for weeks on end, and then the next month I could do every school drop and pickup. It makes it very hard for you to plan your own work/career.

I would love to work less now though and do more at home. I would have no problem with me retiring and you being the breadwinner. That's how the relationship started isn't it? I would love that to be the way it ends.

Could you be the default parent? Why/why not?

Rob: I could be, but I would, in your opinion, be bad at it as we have different ideas and priorities. I have offered to pack the kids' suitcases for holiday every time we go away and you always say no.

I do think that sometimes the default parent can struggle to hand over control.

But, for me to be the full-time default parent, I couldn't work as much as I do. Last year, I was away for work for 112 nights. That's one third of the year, which puts a huge amount of pressure on you to do everything and be the default. I couldn't do it and keep working like I am.

So physically you'd struggle to be the default as you're away a lot, but what about the mental default-ness? Do you think you could cope with the mental load of it all?

Rob: I would massively struggle with it, but I'd have to treat it like a job, but that would mean I couldn't do my job as well. Or not properly anyway. Because being a default parent is like a full-time job, so I couldn't do two full-time jobs properly; I'd be stretched too thin. Even if I didn't travel all the time and was at home more, I don't think I could keep on top of everything I'd need to do if I was working and being in charge of all the parenting things.

What do you think I do all day?

Rob: You worry for most of it. Thinking, constantly thinking, about what the kids need and what's coming up. There's also a lot of coffee and Pilates in the mix alongside writing this book though. But mostly worrying and planning.

Do you think you could cope without me?

Rob: If I stopped working then I could, yes, but it would be fucking chaos and the girls would start to be in charge very quickly. If I was still working like I am now then there's no way I could cope at all. I think I would have to employ about five nannies.

Lou: *To clarify, this isn't a morbid 'if I died' question, I meant it more like imagine I mysteriously disappeared or had to go away for work for ages, etc. You could absolutely cope – you're a brilliant dad and perfectly capable adult human being. I just think there'd be a really horrific transition phase where every time something new happened the shit would hit the fan. The girls' birthday parties would happen, for example, but would be booked out of what's available the week before, with none of the 'unnecessary' frills that I add to my to-do list. It wouldn't be that the girls ever went without because you wouldn't let that happen, but I think perhaps the planning and preparation stages of anything you did would be abandoned. You're much better at outsourcing and asking for help than I am though, so I think you'd only let it be chaos once, and then the next year you'd have a party planner on it and devolve the responsibility to someone else, whereas I'm the other way: I actively make my life more difficult than it needs to be sometimes by insisting on doing it myself.*

Would you have given up work if I'd gone back? Did you think about it?

Rob: Never thought about it for a second due to the career trajectory I was on. Seemed like that would have been a bad decision. But if we both had office jobs and you earned more money than me I would have suggested being a stay-at-home dad.

If we were on the same money, then I would have suggested a discussion about it.

If I went away and did no preparation, what would happen? You said the other week, 'I thought all our alarms went off at 6.45', but everyone else is up, dressed, fed and bags packed by then. What do you think was happening?

Rob: No, this is where we could fall out. If you went away, I would be able to cope – I would make some mistakes at the start then learn.

I would get up later than you.

I think you get up too early in the morning. But that's personal preference. You work best with preparation time and structure. I work well in chaos.

Remember when the flights got cancelled to Orlando everyone was freaking out and I was super calm?

I love you more than anything, but I fundamentally disagree with how you get ready for a day.

Lou: *I think this goes back to, yes, you work well in chaos and you very much lean into 'I'll sort it out when it happens, no point worrying about it now', but I think you're able to do that for yourself because there's only one of you. I'm organising three of us, so if I wake up later, then I'm trying to get three people up and out the door without screaming, which is three times harder than just getting myself up and out. Same with packing for holidays: if I pack for myself badly or forget something, it's not the end of the world because that only impacts me. If I pack the wrong stuff for the girls and have to constantly go and find replacements for the stuff I've forgotten on holiday then it's stressful for all of us and impacts the whole day.*

Rob (insisting on a second right of reply): LET ME TRY!

Do you think you lean into the assumption I'm responsible? You'll do it if I ask you, but if I didn't ask, at what point would you think you needed to do it?

Rob: Yes, I do, but I think that's because our current set-up is I work full time and you're the full-time parent at home. However, we are in a pivot year so we need to have a sit-down discussion about the new roles and responsibilities going forward. When I go away, do you remember to put the bins out if I don't remind you?

Lou: *The fact that, out of all the family/house jobs, Rob only has putting out the bins to hold over me is telling to be honest.*

Women multitask for an extra 10 hours a week compared to men, which leads to stress/conflict/psychological distress – thoughts?

Rob: I believe that to be true, but, in my experience with you, there are some tasks that you are doing that don't need to be done. For example, birthday presents for a school friend. I'd just put a tenner in a card and not think about it again. That would free up a couple of hours of multitasking at least.

Lou: *I feel like he's deliberately missing the point here, to be honest. It's not whether the task is necessary or not, it's that the women or defaults in the dynamic are having to do more mental and physical tasks than their partners, which eats into their leisure and relaxing time. Perhaps the non-defaults have to, at least in part, persuade themselves that a lot of the tasks we're completing are unnecessary or optional to absolve themselves of the responsibility or guilt at not doing these tasks? Tasks that we all know are perhaps not vital, but necessary.*

Rob (again, insisting on a second right of reply): Define 'necessary'. I rest my case, your honour.

Women do almost double the childcare in every area (managerial, physical and educational) apart from recreation, so dads get to do more of the fun stuff. Is that the reason why I'm always more stressed than you?

Rob: Well, the girls ask you to do the fun stuff, getting in the pool on holiday, etc., but you do refuse at times.

I think because, when it comes to recreation time, the default wants a rest away from the kids so they miss out on the fun stuff.

Also, most men are stupid and will do stupid things that the kids like.

Lou: *I take his point here – that he's more up for the silly stuff, and I'm definitely guilty of letting Rob take the lead on holiday with pool stuff (apart from water sports, which I take the hit on because Rob feels about water sports as he does about roller coasters: he hates them) as, after some solid default parenting, I deserve to sit and read my book. But it's more than who gets in the pool on holiday. And, for the record, I do get in – I've dragged myself around Go Apes, half drowned myself down the rapids at Center Parcs and thrown myself around Ninja Warrior obstacle courses with the best of them. It's more than that. It's easier to be Fun-Time Frankie when you're swerving most of the naggy logistics of family life. If I'm swerving playing monsters in the pool on holiday, I think I've earned that for all the time I've spent fruitlessly yelling up the stairs to 'BRUSH YOUR TEETH'.*

When it comes to the girls' parties, days out and so on, you often say I overbook us, borrow trouble unnecessarily, but if I didn't, would it get done?

Rob: Certain things like birthdays need to be organised and planned in advance. But I do think you overbook us in activities and social activities. I prefer a more last-minute plan.

Lou: *Without sounding really patronising, I think this difference in our approaches comes from lived experience of being in charge of the girls for the majority of their free time versus the minority. It's relatively easy to spontaneously fill a day at the last minute and not lose your marbles if things are booked up or their mates aren't available. It's a very different story when you've got weeks and weeks of school holidays to fill. Or even just a whole weekend, devoid of structure. The novelty wears off really quickly by the ninth time you've been told, 'I'm bored.' I find it so much easier if I have plans. Spontaneity gets old real quick when you've got two bored, aggy children in tow. You need a plan; you need many, many plans.*

Do you think I respect your opinion on family logistics, etc.?

Rob: I don't think you really respect my opinion on anything you've already decided on. Luckily, we agree most of the time anyway. If I offer my opinion on any interior design in the house, you say, 'We'll see', which means we won't see and you've already ordered the furniture you've just this second asked my opinion on.

Lou: *Fair. Absolutely fair. Without being nauseating, we do tend to broadly agree on things to do with the girls. There's very rarely something that I'd say yes to, and Rob no, or vice versa. I do run a bit roughshod over Rob's opinion about house things or stuff I've already organised for the girls, which isn't that I don't* *respect his opinion or care what he thinks, it's just that I've spent so much more of my time thinking about what's wrong with the living room rug, or what would make a really fun day out, because I'm not spending my time thinking about what would make a good episode of* Rob & Romesh. *So we're approaching these discussions from totally different perspectives. When I ask him what he thinks, he's approaching it as a new issue that's just occurred to him, whereas I'm already three hours, two self-imagined crises and a solution in.*

If I wanted to broach something about our division of labour, how would you best receive that?

Rob: Just tell me straight up. Honesty is the best policy. That's the quickest way to solving a problem – just being honest about it.

Like any problem in any relationship, you need to talk to your partner and be honest about how you feel and what you want to change. Then you can work towards improving it together. Or, if you are uncomfortable having that kind of chat, write a blog and get a book deal so your partner gets the fucking message.

Is there anything you think we should try differently or you will do differently? Either in terms of parenting or our relationship?

Rob: I am happy to work less and do more at home, even if that means a drop in finances. I value everyone in the home being happy and content with improved self-worth over a new car or bottle of champagne at a restaurant.

Lou: *I do not. Keep going to work. I like being a Pilates princess and I refuse to surrender it now.*

So, there we have it – Rob's right of reply. What I think I can take from this is that, while we clearly have had very different experiences of parenting, he does understand, as far as it's possible to as a non-default, just how hard it can be being the one in charge. What I've also learnt is just how thoroughly different Rob and I are as parents. Which I obviously knew as I've lived with his maddeningly chipper 'It'll be fine, you worry too much' attitude to organisation for long enough, but it hits differently hearing him say it in so much detail. How much of that is just our different personalities versus default/non-default roles is up for debate, but, betwixt the two of us, we muddle through.

It's also really validating to hear him say how much I took the hit as the default parent, and how much his career and identity took precedence over mine in the early days. Even with the benefit of hindsight, I wouldn't change what we did, but maybe I would have spoken about the decisions we were making more and why we were making them. Our communication was great before kids, but effectively fell off a cliff when we first had our eldest because, in Rob's words, our lives fell into a proper 'kick bollock scramble' for a while. We've clawed back some calm amid the chaos as the girls have got older though and, if our parenting/relationship journey demonstrates anything, it's that, yes, your communication can take a real hit when you have kids because you're just stretched too thin, but everything gets better eventually – but you've got to talk about it.

FINAL WORDS

IF I'VE LEARNT ANYTHING

(And I'm Not Sure I Have)

So, we've firmly established that, as the mums, and especially the defaults, we're working harder, and that this is outrageously unfair. There's absolutely no getting around the fact that the burden of having children falls massively and disproportionately on to the woman in the first instance and then whoever assumes that default role in the second. I can't solve this conundrum for you – no one can. Short of availing yourself of every marvel of modern science and employing a veritable team of staff to absorb some of the new parenting workload, there's just no getting around the fact that your life is seismically different to how it was before kids. Even if you could utilise science and staff to share the weight of having and raising children, there would still be the omnipresent spectre of guilt to contend with.

What I think I've really come to fully appreciate while writing this book is just how much as defaults we both take on and expect of ourselves. When I wrote out a list of all the physical and mental jobs I complete for the family, it was genuinely overwhelming. When you actually stop and calculate how much you're being expected to do, how much pressure you're putting on yourself to do it all and do it all right, just how many things you have going on at any single time, then is it any surprise some of us are struggling to manage?

When you apply for a job, you have to tell them what experience you have, but there's no prior experience that's massively applicable for having a baby, for forging a new identity overnight, for being expected to fulfil a totally different space in your family dynamic than you ever have before. It can be completely unmooring to be thrust into these new responsibilities without preparation.

To feel a bit shit at your job is a horrible feeling. Imagine feeling like that all the time. I felt really, really shit at my new-mum job when I first got it. I couldn't feed my daughter. I didn't know what she needed. I didn't know the answer to anything, unless that answer was 'phone my mum and ask her to come round and help'. That feeling of inadequacy doesn't go away – it evolves into different forms, but it's always there. Inadequate as a mother. As a partner. As a career woman. As a friend. As anything really because you're simply being stretched too thin to be effective. Never have I identified more with that pathetic little smear of butter at the bottom of the tub as I frantically try to spread it across my 8-year-old's toast at 6.30am. We all know in our heart of hearts that there's not enough and we need a new tub, but we keep going scraping at the plastic because we forgot to buy any more.

So, what's the answer? If we're agreeing that, in different ways for all of us, after having babies and becoming the de facto default parent, the pegs of our lives don't match the holes they used to, if we can't entirely square the circle, how do we round off the corners at least? How do we soften the impact and reclaim some of our 'us-ness'? How do we re-centre ourselves as a priority without feeling like a selfish arsehole?

Be Honest with Yourself and Others

I feel like I've learnt so much about my own feelings just laying it all out here in one place. It's brought up emotions I don't think I was fully aware of at the time and, in hindsight, maybe that's half the problem – I didn't have the mental or physical space to check in on myself, so allowed those feelings and experiences to fester, and resentments to take root, that could probably have been avoided or at least mitigated. I've felt sadness, anger and frustration, but also so much happiness and love in revisiting my parenting journey so far. I wasn't expecting to feel such a full spectrum of emotions in looking backwards, but what's clear is that there was a lot of deep-seated frustration that I've let linger for far too long, because I haven't addressed it earlier. Nothing terrible has happened, obviously – we haven't experienced any trauma, Rob and I are still happily married and we have a very contented life as a little Gang of Four, but, in some ways, I'm quite sad when I look back at Lou of 10 years ago, absolutely losing her marbles and feeling like the worst mum in the world, because there was just no need. I absolutely am not, and was not, a bad mum. I just didn't know what I was doing and I hadn't been prepared for the incoming full-scale identity crisis and overwhelm of default parenthood.

There's no amount of checking in or discussion that's going to return you to your pre-baby self, but I think I would have been able to develop and embrace my new identity much less bumpily if I'd been a bit more honest with myself and Rob about what I was struggling with. I also think that it's immeasurably useful for us to share our experiences and be receptive to hearing about others in a way that we don't feel the need to pass judgement or get defensive. Having children, becoming a parent, being the default, is so entrenched in society that we've normalised the enormity of the changes that come with that. Just because it's happening to lots of people, it doesn't mean that it's not a massive, huge, impactful thing. We're allowed to go, 'What in actual fuck is happening to me?' without feeling like failures, because, I'm sorry, what the actual fuck is a lot of pregnancy and parenthood? It's BONKERS that we all just go, 'Oh, OK that's happening now, cool, cool' and crack on.

Talk to yourself. By hook or by crook you have to find some mental capacity to check in with yourself sometimes. That's going to look different for everyone. Maybe your mum watches the kids for a few hours every so often, maybe you get the babies on a bottle so Dad can feed them and you take the opportunity once in a while to get a full sanity-restoring eight hours' sleep. Maybe that's you and your partner going for a walk with the pram and getting some fresh air and perspective. (It's hard to get perspective when you haven't left the living room for three days.) Personally, I joined the gym down the road from our old house, ostensibly to 'bounce back' (still working on the old bounce back almost a decade later, but we move), but realistically what I did more than anything else was throw the girls into the crèche there and sit in the café in silence nursing a coffee while trying to restore myself to a level of something approaching sanity. You need time to gather together the threads of you again and, while there isn't a monetary value placed on your time if you're a stay-at-home parent, or the default, that time still needs to be a priority.

Your partner, much as we'd like them to be, isn't a mind reader. Absolutely, yes, they should be able to assess a situation and appreciate that there have been some ground-shiftingly massive changes to your life, and, while theirs has returned in many ways to normal, yours hasn't yet. In an ideal world and as a fully-grown adult, *of course*, they should be identifying that you might be struggling and they should be proactively trying to divide that load more equitably, but we're after solutions not ideals here. Instead of getting resentful and frustrated that they don't know how we're feeling and what we need, we need to communicate this.

Admittedly, it's very hard to communicate sometimes – it's hard to articulate how we feel in this entirely new and emotive situation because we simply don't know ourselves. That doesn't mean that we shouldn't try, however. If you're at the point of your parenting journey where you're not pregnant or a parent yet, then now is the time to set those precedents. Set up the framework for you to have that communication with your partner. *How are you feeling? Do you need anything from me? This is how I feel. This is what I need.* It's also never too late to open those channels of communication. Something Rob and I have started doing after many conversations that, despite our best efforts, ended up feeling quite fraught, is asking each other what our capacity is. *What does your week look like? Do you have the capacity to take on XYZ?* Tell your partner how you're feeling and what you need. You're not going to get all of it because no one has all the answers, time or money needed to do that – like I appreciate I can't simply leave the kids with my mum and take myself off to Orlando to ride Tower of Terror every time I feel sad, but I can ask Rob to take the girls to their weekend clubs when he's not working to give me one day a week when I'm not on someone else's timetable, which went a long way to making me feel like an independent person again.

Mind Your Language

I'm no NLP aficionado, but there's a lot of power in the language you use. If you're not sure what it is, because, beyond TikTok clips, I'm not sure either to be honest, then NLP is defined by the Association for NLP as: 'Neuro linguistic programming comprises models, techniques and strategies to help us understand how the language we use influences the way we think and the results we get.'[1] In its most simplistic form, it's using language to positively change the way we think and to achieve the results we want.

As much as I'd love to tell you how to mind-trick your partner into becoming the perfect Stepford husband, this is more about you as the default being really mindful about the language you're using about yourself and your life.

Maybe the non-defaults in our lives wouldn't be so entrenched in that understanding of their responsibilities if we didn't frame them in such an optional way. The assumption of a shared responsibility, or an unassigned responsibility, is really powerful. Think about how you would arrange the following situation with the non-default in your life:

Your children have clubs on a weekend. Both you and your partner are free and at home that day. Is there any discussion about who's taking them? If you couldn't or didn't want to take them for whatever reason, how would that be phrased to your partner? Would it be, 'Can you take them for me?' If it's a 'can you …?' or a 'for me', then you're asking for a favour. You are allowing the assumption that you're responsible unless you've asked someone else to be. How often does your partner ask you if you 'can' be responsible for whatever child/family activity it is? Remove the assumption of responsibility from you as the default. Obviously, I'm not saying you have to or should ask about every single thing that needs doing on a daily basis. Rob doesn't expect me to go and do one of his tour shows for him, because that's his job and responsibility. And, if I did, people would quite understandably be very confused and ask for a refund. Likewise, I don't expect him to do the things that are my job in the house/family. The grey areas, however, which are much bigger and greyer in reality once you look critically at the division of responsibility, are absolutely a shared load. Or they should be. For those tasks, don't ask, 'Can you?', ask, 'Who is going to?' Put the onus on that task being an unassigned and shared job. If they can't/don't want to, ask for a reason.

Most of our partners are not lazy, selfish arseholes who revel in making us take on the lion's share of the load. More often than not, they've simply not thought about it because no one's expected them to. Unless someone tells them otherwise, or prompts that reflection, why would they mess with a system that works, for them at least? So just ask the question. Don't assume the responsibility. You don't have to charge in there all guns blazing demanding answers as to why they're a lazy shit. Just pose the question, and don't be afraid of following up with more questions. Start from the expectation of shared responsibility. If we want things to change, then we have to allow our partners the opportunity to be more involved.

I also try to avoid taking on the task of problem-solving for my entire family now. Loath as I am to admit that I'm anything less than an omniscient being, the all-powerful matriarch of my household, I have really leant into the power of simply saying, 'I don't know.' I try, as much as is practical, to match their level of effort. If the entire sum of all their efforts to solve a problem or find an answer is to ask me, then I'm very much meeting them where they're at. The default (pun intended) reaction to not knowing something, or not finding something, or needing something, is to hit me up. Mummy'll know. Rob is absolutely included in this, by the way. If there's no real reason why I should know the answer more than anyone else in this conversation, then I simply say, 'I don't know.' If the information is accessible to all of us, then I try to not make myself the sole conduit of knowledge in my household. 'I don't know, have you checked the chart on the wall?', 'I'm not sure, have you checked the emails from school?', 'No idea, have you looked?' You're not being mean or setting anyone up to fail; see it more that you're giving them the opportunity to develop. You're empowering them to do it themselves. I feel the same way about answering stupid questions, or solving solvable problems for my family (mostly Rob, to be honest, as the girls are still young enough to just about get away with it). If the information is accessible, you don't need to be their access to it; let them work it out.

As a follow-up to this, and try not to be too aghast as I undo all that good work our mothers did in our childhoods teaching us to say thank you at the end of every feasible sentence, but don't say thank you. I know, shock and horror abound! Don't thank the non-default for things that they don't need thanking for. This one is especially key if you're trying to untangle a lot of the default systems and assumptions of responsibility that have become quite entrenched in your family dynamic.

I'm not saying to march around your house demanding your partner do things and never be grateful, but if we're trying to unpick the concept that you're responsible for all the things all the time, then we have to stop thanking our partners for things we aren't being thanked for. Remove the illusion that they are doing you a favour by helping you. They're not helping you; they're doing their fair share for the children and the family that is just as much theirs as yours. This is much easier to do when the question itself is reframed as a 'Who's doing XYZ' instead of 'Can you do XYZ for me?' If you haven't asked for something like you're asking for a favour, then it feels much less rude to not follow it up with misplaced gratitude.

Gratitude is a tricky thing for women especially. All children, but girls in particular I think, are taught to be polite, kind and absolutely grateful. This translates over into our adult relationships, both at work and otherwise. In my experience, you've only got to look at women's work emails in comparison to men's – we say statements as questions to soften their impact in case people think we're demanding, we caveat our opinions and ideas lest we seem cocky and we express gratitude so much more often than our male counterparts.

This isn't me telling you to go on a one-woman feminist crusade against the men in your life and never express any gratitude ever again, because, quite frankly, that'd make you altogether a pretty unpleasant person to be around, but there's absolutely nothing wrong with being very mindful and intentional in how we frame both our requests *and* our responses. It's uncomfortable to begin with. I felt I sounded so ungrateful and very cold when I first started trying to implement this kind of language in my discussions with Rob over house/family issues – it made the conversations feel quite transactional at times. However, and it's a big however, it's also incredibly powerful once you learn to just sit with that feeling. Just let it be. Let the silence hang and resist the temptation to jump into the void and solve the problem. I feel so much more empowered when I'm meeting Rob conversationally from a point of equality. I'm not asking for a favour; instead, we're working together as partners to split the load and determine what's going to be best for *all* of us.

I don't have to do this as consciously anymore, and I certainly say thank you to Rob many times a day, because we've now established that precedent for our conversations where we're both approaching it from a 'Who is going to do what this week?' perspective.

By holding the line and approaching the conversations differently, I've been able to adjust the parameters of our roles into something that functions much more effectively for the whole family.

Ultimately, and I know this isn't the answer anyone wants, there is no easy way through being a parent, and certainly not through being the default parent. What I can unequivocally say is that it is 110 per cent worth it. If it means I get to have my delicious girls, my bonkers little gang, then sign me up. I'll take identity crises, breastfeeding breakdowns and the almost irrepressible urges to punch Rob or myself in the face a hundred times over if I get to have them. Just because it's worth the hard work, though, if we can make it less hard work then why shouldn't we? If we can, and WE CAN, have all the good without so much of the bad, then that can only be a good thing, right? You're never going to be able to plan, or talk, or NLP your way around the impacts of default parenthood, but you can mitigate a hell of a lot of it by being honest with yourself and your partner about what you're feeling and what you need. Don't be afraid or ashamed to speak up if you're struggling in whatever way, big or small – none of this is happening without you; you are just as important in your family dynamic as any of the other parts. Advocate for yourself the way you'd advocate for your best friend in a break-up.

Also know that you're not alone. Becoming a mother and then occupying the default parent role can feel really overwhelming. Not all the time, but enough of the time to have an impact. If you feel completely unmoored, then please know that that's so normal. People don't talk about it enough and most people, on the outside at least, look like they're coping marvellously, so we expect to be able to launch ourselves into our new lives as default parent seamlessly. While it might work for some people, there are more of us out there on the struggle bus than I think we appreciate.

Our partners might never get it fully, and that's OK. How could they? There's a huge community of defaults out there, however, who do absolutely see you. Who know how hard you're working to be the best parent that you can be.

I know you're an incredible parent. You wouldn't be worrying so much unless you cared. I also know you have so much more to give than solely being a parent. That doesn't make you a bad parent – it just means you are a person beyond parenthood. Which is a good thing. If it's hard now, then it won't always be. You don't have to be doing it perfectly, all the time, to be doing your best, and your best is bloody amazing.

Most of all ... Solidarity to the defaults.

NOTES

Introduction: The Mother of All Caveats

1. Collins, 2025. Definition of 'default'. Retrieved from www.collinsdictionary.com/dictionary/english/default.
2. Gov.uk, 15 Jan. 2021. Sharing of childcare and well-being outcomes: An empirical analysis. Retrieved from www.gov.uk/government/publications/childcare-shared-care-and-well-being-outcomes-for-families/sharing-of-childcare-and-well-being-outcomes-an-empirical-analysis.
3. Weeks, A. C. and Ruppanner, L., 2025. A typology of US parents' mental loads: Core and episodic cognitive labor. *Journal of Marriage and Family*, 87(3), pp. 966–89.
4. Hytten, F., 1985. Blood volume changes in normal pregnancy. *Clinics in Haematology*, *14*(3), pp. 601–12.

1: The Parent Trap (And Not the Fun One with Lindsay Lohan)

1. Kearns, R. J., Kyzayeva, A., Halliday, L. O., Lawlor, D. A., Shaw, M. and Nelson, S. M., 2024. Epidural analgesia during labour and severe maternal morbidity: Population based study. *BMJ*, 385.

2: Who Am I Now? (Life with a Newborn)

1. Gov.uk, 17 Nov. 2016. UK gender pay gap. Retrieved from www.gov.uk/government/news/uk-gender-pay-gap.
2. Wigert, B. and Pendell, R., 16 Dec. 2024. 7 workplace challenges for 2025. GALLUP. Retrieved from www.gallup.com/workplace/654329/workplace-challenges-2025.aspx.

3. University of Bath, 7 Mar. 2025. Mothers bear the brunt of the 'mental load,' managing 7 in 10 household tasks. Retrieved from www.bath.ac.uk/announcements/mothers-bear-the-brunt-of-the-mental-load-managing-7-in-10-household-tasks/#:~:text=Key%20Findings,much%20as%20dads%20(37%25).
4. Davis, N., 26 Feb. 2019. New parents face up to six years of sleep deprivation, study says. *The Guardian*. Retrieved from https://amp.theguardian.com/lifeandstyle/2019/feb/26/parenthood-sleep-deprivation-after-birth-mothers-hit-hardest-research.
5. Venn, S., Arber, S., Meadows, R. and Hislop, J., 2008. The fourth shift: Exploring the gendered nature of sleep disruption among couples with children. *The British Journal of Sociology*, 59(1), pp. 79–97.
6. Division of Sleep Medicine, 1 Oct. 2021. Why sleep matters: Consequences of sleep deficiency. Harvard Medical School. Retrieved from https://sleep.hms.harvard.edu/education-training/public-education/sleep-and-health-education-program/sleep-health-education-45.
7. Gordon, A. M. and Chen, S., 2014. The role of sleep in interpersonal conflict: Do sleepless nights mean worse fights? *Social Psychological and Personality Science*, 5(2), pp. 168–75.
8. Berkowitz, G., Jan. 2025. UCLA study on friendship among women. Women's Brain Health Initiative. Retrieved from womensbrainhealth.org/think-tank/think-twice/ucla-study-on-friendship-among-women; Crooks, V. C., Lubben, J., Petitti, D.., Little, D. and Chiu, V., 2008. Social network, cognitive function, and dementia incidence among elderly women. *American Journal of Public Health*, 98(7), pp. 1221–7.

6: Remember You're on the Same Team

1. University of Bath, Mothers bear the brunt of the 'mental load,' managing 7 in 10 household tasks.

7: *Can You Have It All?*

1. Offer, S. and Schneider, B., 2011. Revisiting the gender gap in time-use patterns: Multitasking and well-being among mothers and fathers in dual-earner families. *American Sociological Review*, 76(6), pp. 809–33.
2. Ibid.
3. Weeks, A. C. and Ruppanner, L., A typology of US parents' mental loads: Core and episodic cognitive labor.
4. Daminger, A., 2019. The cognitive dimension of household labor. *American Sociological Review*, 84(4), pp. 609–33.
5. Szameitat, A. J., Hamaida, Y., Tulley, R. S., Saylik, R. and Otermans, P. C., 2015. 'Women are better than men' – Public beliefs on gender differences and other aspects in multitasking. *PLOS One*, 10(10), p. e0140371.
6. Bianchi, S. M. and Mattingly, M. J., 2003. 5. Time, work and family in the United States. *Advances in Life Course Research*, 8, pp. 95–118.
7. Wang, W., 17 Oct. 2013. The 'leisure gap' between mothers and fathers. Pew Research Center. Retrieved from www.pewresearch.org/short-reads/2013/10/17/the-leisure-gap-between-mothers-and-fathers/#:~:text=In%20America%2C%20fathers%2C%20on%20average,least%20over%20the%20past%20decade.
8. Wang, W., 8 Oct. 2013. Parents' time with kids more rewarding than paid work – and more exhausting. Pew Research Center. Retrieved from www.pewresearch.org/social-trends/2013/10/08/parents-time-with-kids-more-rewarding-than-paid-work-and-more-exhausting.
9. Gov.uk, Sharing of childcare and well-being outcomes: An empirical analysis.
10. Weeks, A. C. and Ruppanner, L., A typology of US parents' mental loads: Core and episodic cognitive labor.
11. Offer, S. and Schneider, B., Revisiting the gender gap in time-use patterns: Multitasking and well-being among mothers and fathers in dual-earner families.

12. Szameitat, A. J., Hamaida, Y., Tulley, R. S., Saylik, R. and Otermans, P. C., 'Women are better than men' – Public beliefs on gender differences and other aspects in multitasking.
13. Bianchi, S. M. and Mattingly, M. J., 5. Time, work and family in the United States.
14. Wang, W., The 'leisure gap' between mothers and fathers.
15. Wang, W., Parents' time with kids more rewarding than paid work – and more exhausting.
16. Davis, N., New parents face up to six years of sleep deprivation, study says.
17. Gordon, A. M. and Chen, S., The role of sleep in interpersonal conflict: Do sleepless nights mean worse fights?

Final Words: If I've Learnt Anything (And I'm Not Sure I Have)

1. The Association for NLP, 2025. Definition of NLP. Retrieved from anlp.org/knowledge-base/definition-of-nlp.

ACKNOWLEDGEMENTS

To my girls – you two are bonkers, stubborn, creative, beautiful, strong, hysterical, imaginative, frustrating, loving, ridiculous and a thousand other adjectives in equal measure. I love you more than anything. There is nothing more important to me than being your mum. Whatever else I've said about being a parent here, there is nothing and no one I love more than the pair of you. The fanny club, as Daddy calls us, is my favourite thing in the world – you're my little best mates and I will be your cheerleader, supporter and friend for as long as I live, and I may well haunt you from the beyond as well. I can't wait to see you continue to grow up into the most amazing ladies. You're going to change the world, I know it. Team vagina forever.

Rob, none of this would be possible without you. You're my best friend and I love you. I knew you'd be an amazing dad, but I couldn't have imagined just how brilliant you'd be. All your hard work, the long days/weeks of filming and the sacrifices you make for us do not go unnoticed, and we three appreciate it more than you know. Your support for writing this book has been invaluable. You've believed in me when I didn't believe in myself, just like you always have. Our little gang is my favourite thing in the world and I hope our adventures continue forever.

To my parents, Teresa and Mike (feels weird to use your proper names), thank you for everything. In what I've realised is the eternal cycle of parenthood, I didn't appreciate when I was younger just how much hard work you were both putting in continually to give us the kind of halcyon childhood we had. And I will be forever grateful. It's testament to you both, and just how much all three of us love you, that you've never quite got rid of any of us. We still need you just as much as we ever did. You're the best, silliest, most loving Nana and Amps. I wouldn't be half as healthy, happy and sane as I am without your support, and you allowing me to shamelessly abuse your babysitting generosity.

My sisters Rhi and Beth – I love you so much and thank you for being family that feels like friends.

It takes a village, and Lisa babysitter, you're our village MVP (most valuable player). Thank you for looking after the girls like they're your own – I'm so grateful to have your help.

There's a whole collection of people who I couldn't do life without, friends who feel like family: Sam, Kate, Shell, Laura, Pumps and Nat – 20 years and going strong; The Bundle, I love you; Hayley and Andy, the most loving and fun people I know; Jess and Jey, we'll always have the Metro; Tom Allen, you're a constant source of support, laughter and love; and Lisa and Vicky, my breakout WhatsApp partners in crime. Your collective support for this book, your friendship, the talking down from spirals, the relentless yapping, the wine drinking, the holiday booking, the Pilates motivation and obscene coffee consumption has kept me sane – I love you all so much.

Danny, thank you for having my back and allowing me to co-opt you as my agent without actually asking if it was OK. Your support and belief through this process has meant more than you know. Rob and I both owe you so much, and we're very grateful to have you in our corner.

Everyone at DK, especially the powerhouses that are Lucy and Elizabeth. Thank you for reading the blog post, for believing it could be a book and championing it to fruition. It means so much. Julia, editor extraordinaire, you made the last push so much more manageable when the words no longer made sense to me and I'm very grateful.

Lastly, to everyone who read the original blog post and shared, commented or messaged. Thank you for making me feel seen. This book quite literally wouldn't be here without your support. I didn't appreciate how unmoored from myself I felt, and while writing this book and putting myself out there like this is, quite frankly, terrifying, I hadn't appreciated how validating it would also be. Thank you for giving me that.